THE CUSTOMS UNION ISSUE

Jacob Viner

EDITED AND WITH AN
INTRODUCTION BY
Paul Oslington

OXFORD
UNIVERSITY PRESS

OXFORD
UNIVERSITY PRESS

Oxford University Press is a department of the University of Oxford.
It furthers the University's objective of excellence in research, scholarship,
and education by publishing worldwide.

Oxford   New York
Auckland   Cape Town   Dar es Salaam   Hong Kong   Karachi
Kuala Lumpur   Madrid   Melbourne   Mexico City   Nairobi
New Delhi   Shanghai   Taipei   Toronto

With offices in
Argentina   Austria   Brazil   Chile   Czech Republic   France   Greece
Guatemala   Hungary   Italy   Japan   Poland   Portugal   Singapore
South Korea   Switzerland   Thailand   Turkey   Ukraine   Vietnam

Oxford is a registered trademark of Oxford University Press
in the UK and certain other countries.

Published in the United States of America by
Oxford University Press
198 Madison Avenue, New York, NY 10016

© Oxford University Press 2014

Library of Congress Cataloging-in-Publication Data
Viner, Jacob, 1892–1970.
The customs union issue / Jacob Viner ; edited, with an Introduction by Paul Oslington.
pages cm
Includes bibliographical references and index.
ISBN 978-0-19-975612-4 (alk. paper)
1. Customs unions.   I. Oslington, Paul.   II. Title.
HF1713.V52 2013
382'.91—dc23
2013010509

1 3 5 7 9 8 6 4 2
Printed in the United States of America
on acid-free paper

CONTENTS

FOREWORD TO THE 1950 EDITION

GEORGE A. FINCH

Carnegie Endowment for International Peace

Among the projects undertaken by the Carnegie Endowment during the war years under its program of providing materials which would be helpful in the solution of postwar problems was that of making available information regarding the arrangements and experience of customs unions. A collection of some 250 or more documents, beginning with the Germans' Zollverein and including some proposals for customs unions which did not materialize, was assembled in original English texts or in English translation.

Dr. Jacob Viner, outstanding economist and author, on the basis of a critical examination and study of the texts thus made available and experience in connection with past unions, offers the present study as an attempt to throw some light on the possibilities and the limitations of customs unions as a method of regulating international commercial relations. Formerly Professor of Economics of the University of Chicago, Dr. Viner is now with the Department of Economics and Social Institutions of Princeton University. He has also been associated with the United States Tariff Commission, the United States Shipping

Board, and the Treasury Department, and since 1943 has served as consultant to the Department of State. He speaks with authority, and his study is a challenging contribution to the discussion of this timely subject.

In view of the unique value of the collection of documents, the present study is supplemented by a list of the customs union treaties, conventions, and decrees included in the collection, with source references. A comprehensive bibliography completes the work. The collection, in typewritten form, is available for consultation in the Library of the Endowment.

The present volume constitutes the tenth and concluding number of the Endowment's series of "Studies in the Administration of International Law and Organization."

George A. Finch
Former Director of the Division of International Law
Washington DC
January 3, 1950

PREFACE

GENE GROSSMAN

Jacob Viner Professor of International Economics,
Princeton University

It is a pleasure and an honor to write this preface to the new issuance of Jacob Viner's classic work, edited by Paul Oslington. As the Jacob Viner Professor of International Economics, I am an avid collector of all of Viner's writings. My copy of *The Customs Union Issue* is well worn, so this new printing will find a welcome home on my bookshelf. For those who are not collectors like me, the availability of this new issuance will be even more valuable. The questions that Viner addresses have only grown in importance since the time of the book's writing, and some of his insights are no less keen and relevant today than they were in their day. It is fascinating to read of trade creation and trade diversion from their original source and to discover what Viner did and did not actually say in the book after so much ink has been spilled on the subject. Much as with other reprinted classics, it will immediately be clear that the author's treatment of his subject is much richer than the catchphrase terms that have become associated with it.

Paul Oslington's introduction is fascinating. This is not surprising from one so well versed in both international trade theory and the history of economic thought. I had the pleasure to interact with Paul and watch as he painstakingly conducted the archival research that informs and enlivens his introduction. The introduction spells out the context for the book's writing, the literature that predated it, and the influence that Viner's contemporaries had on his thinking about preferential trading arrangements. Also fascinating is Oslington's discussion of the criticisms that followed the publication of the book and Viner's responses to them. These responses, often in personal correspondence between Viner and his critics, were uncovered by Oslington in his foray into the Mudd Manuscript Library at Princeton University, where Viner's personal papers are stored.

Oslington's introduction also is endearing for its disarming honesty. The editor clearly admires the work that he seeks to return to the public eye, but he is hardly fawning in his praise. To the contrary, he openly discusses Viner's lack of clarity about his assumptions and the fact that modern authors cite Viner's work more to establish their own authority on the subject than to engage closely with the analytical arguments it contains. One comes away from the introduction with an understanding of the enduring value of this classic work, but also of its limitations.

It is great to see this project come to fruition. This was a labor of love, and the community of international trade economists owes Paul Oslington a great debt for it. I, for one, look forward to owning and rereading this new issuance and to being reminded that the truly classic works can live beyond the creation of next year's graduate reading list.

ACKNOWLEDGMENTS

This work draws on the Jacob Viner papers held at the Mudd Manuscript Library at Princeton University, and I thank Mudd Librarians Daniel Linke and Adriane Hanson for their assistance with the papers, and the Friends of Princeton University Library for a grant that facilitated this archival work. I appreciate the generous hospitality of Professor Gene Grossman and his colleagues in the International Economics section during the period I was in Princeton working on a number of projects in trade theory, the history of economics, and theology. Warm thanks to Donald Winch, Douglas Irwin, Stephen Meardon, Tony Endres, Jacques Melitz, William Baumol, and Ellen Seiler-Viner for helpful conversations about Viner, and for comments on various parts of my investigation of Viner's work. A biography of Viner is sorely needed.

Terry Vaughn and Scott Parris at Oxford University Press saw the value of making Viner's classic work more readily available to a new generation of economists, and I thank them and Cathryn Vaulman and Catherine Rae for their help through the longer than expected process of bringing it to completion.

INTRODUCTION

PAUL OSLINGTON

Professor of Economics,

Australian Catholic University

Importance of Customs Unions and Other Preferential Trading Arrangements

Explaining the formation of preferential trading arrangements, understanding their effects on the welfare of different groups in different countries and their consequences for the multilateral trade liberalization process, is among the most complex and controversial questions in economics.[1] George Finch of the Carnegie Endowment commented in his foreword to the original issuance of this work that Viner's investigation was timely, and that assessment remains just as true today, if not more so, with the recent proliferation of regional trading arrangements.

---

1. Recent surveys of the economics of preferential trade agreements include Baldwin and Venables (1995), Bhagwati (1993, 2008), Lloyd and Maclaren (2004), Krishna (2008), Panagariya (2000), and Freund and Ornelas (2010). All acknowledge Viner's contribution to the field. Irwin (1993) is an excellent discussion of the history of customs unions up until the mid–twentieth century.

Jacob Viner (1892–1970) was a central figure in twentieth-century economics whose work spanned international economics, price theory, economic policy, and the history of economics.[2] The breadth of his interests and extensive circle of contacts on both sides of the Atlantic led his close friend Lionel Robbins to suggest that the 130 boxes of correspondence and other papers left after his passing would constitute a good history of the profession in the first half of the twentieth century. And his work is impressive not just for its breadth—Viner had a formidable reputation as a theorist despite his lack of mathematical training. This is attested by correspondence with many of the greats of international economics, including Gottfried Haberler, Bertil Ohlin, Frank Graham, Roy Harrod, John Hicks, Paul Samuelson, James Meade, and Max Corden. Samuelson, for instance, sent theoretical papers to Viner for comment from the 1930s up to the early 1960s, and described Viner as "the most celebrated scholar of international economics in our times" and noted the "originality for which he has not pressed claims."[3]

Viner's *The Customs Union Issue,* originally published in 1950, is the one undeniable classic in the field of the economics of preferential trading arrangements.[4] Appreciation of the work began

---

2. General introductions to Jacob Viner's work include Baumol and Viner-Seiler (1979), Winch (1981, 1983), Irwin (1991), Bloomfield (1992), and Groenewegen (1994). There is further biographical material in a paper in progress on Viner's approach to intellectual history (Oslington 2008).

3. Correspondence in the Jacob Viner Papers, Mudd Manuscript Library, Princeton University. The quotations come from a 1969 letter and typescript of Samuelson's 1962 remarks at the American Economic Association annual meeting.

4. Viner's *The Customs Union Issue* remains the most cited work on preferential trading arrangements based on citation counts from Google Scholar for a number of keywords related to preferential trading arrangements. It attracts most citations in economics, but is also frequently cited in international relations, business, and law journals. Among Viner's works *The Customs Union Issue* is his most cited work by a considerable margin, followed by his 1931 article on cost and supply curves, and his 1952 book on international trade and economic development.

with the early reviews, and it quickly became the point of departure for international economists who developed the theory of customs unions. The historian Mark Blaug (1991, p. 298) judged that Viner's book "supplied the starting point for every subsequent work on the economics of common markets and free trade areas." Richard Pomfret (2001, p. 182) lauded Viner as the economist who "made the greatest single contribution to the theory of discriminatory trading arrangements."

The purpose of this introduction is to place Viner's work in context, trace influences on his thinking on customs unions, show what Viner was attempting to do in the book, and consider how it was received.

Context and Influences on Viner's Thinking about Customs Unions

The intellectual commitments and influences on Viner's thinking in the years leading up to the publication of *The Customs Union Issue* are described below in roughly chronological order.[5]

Classical Liberalism and Free Trade

Viner's intellectual commitment to classical liberalism is clear from his published work and correspondence.[6] His early and deep engagement with Adam Smith's moral philosophy, politics, and economics is evident in his classic article (Viner 1937) written for the Chicago celebration of the 150th anniversary of the

---

5. This section on influences and the next on the reception of Viner's work draws on Oslington (2013).

6. Viner's commitment to classical liberalism is further discussed by his longtime friend and fellow liberal Lionel Robbins (1970), and further by Razeen Sally (1998).

publication of *Wealth of Nations*. There are many letters, especially to Alec Macfie and Lionel Robbins, where his continuing admiration for Adam Smith's view of the world is clear, and in a 1967 letter to Bertil Ohlin Viner describes himself as a disciple of Hume. Viner's support for free trade was shown in his Harvard PhD thesis on the classical adjustment mechanism in Canadian trade (Viner 1924a) and continued through his later writings on trade and his work as a policy adviser. His friendship and correspondence encouraged economist colleagues to support the liberal economic order through the dark times of the 1930s and 1940s. He corresponded with Hayek about the formation of the Mont Pelerin Society, although he did not join in the end because he considered that it had become a political organization. Viner's background commitment to a liberal order and free trade was the most important reason for writing *The Customs Union Issue*.

The Classical Economists on Customs Unions

Viner was keenly interested in the history of economic thought from his student days at McGill and Harvard, and aware of discussions of the topic by the classical economists.[7]

The picture sometimes painted in the international trade literature of Viner in 1950 announcing to a stunned world that customs unions are not always beneficial to the countries involved, let alone the world as a whole, is highly questionable. As Denis O'Brien (1976) has documented, this supposedly novel insight that customs unions were not always beneficial was the almost universal understanding of the classical economists. For instance, Adam Smith strongly opposed the Methuen treaty with

---

7. Viner's student records in his papers show he excelled in courses in the history of economic thought at McGill 1911–14 under Stephen Leacock and J. C. Hemmeon and further graduate courses at Harvard from 1914. His book on the early history of international trade theory (Viner 1937) remains unsurpassed.

Portugal signed in 1703, which stipulated that there was to be no tax on Portuguese wines or English textiles. J. R. McCulloch was particularly incensed by the treaty, as it forced him to purchase inferior and more expensive Portuguese wine, rather than French wine. Other treaties, such as the 1860s Cobden-Chevalier Treaty, which included a most-favored-nation (MFN) clause, received support from economists because the benefits of the trade created were believed to exceed the diversion losses, and also because the treaty was thought likely to provoke reductions in general tariff levels.

The writings of the classical economists were an important influence on Viner's work, a stimulus and support for his doubts about preferential trading arrangements.

Taussig and the U.S. Tariff Commission

Viner's interest in preferential trading arrangements seems to have been aroused by his Harvard teacher Frank Taussig, who commented extensively on U.S. trade treaties, especially their reciprocity and most-favored-nation clauses (for instance, Taussig 1892, 1910, 1915) and was generally optimistic about reciprocity arrangements promoting free trade.[8] Taussig's question when assessing reciprocity arrangements was whether they helped or hindered the cause of free trade, and he was sensitive to the problems of American conditional application of the most-favored-nation principle (MFN), though he recognized that there were then few other realistic channels for tariff reduction. Viner learned from Taussig a practical case-by-case approach and the importance of attention to the institutional details of trade agreements. Even

8. Meardon (2011) discusses the Tariff Commission and how Taussig's optimistic view was tempered by subsequent experience. Irwin (1993) provides the larger context.

some of his teacher's specific examples influenced him. Viner's wool and woollen cloth example (Viner 1950, p. 59 [48]) seems based on Taussig's earlier discussion (1910, p. 171).

After Viner had completed his PhD coursework, Taussig arranged for Viner to work in 1917 and 1918 with the U.S. Tariff Commission as a special expert, contributing to its 1919 report *Reciprocity and Commercial Treaties* (United States Tariff Commission 1919—discussed by Meardon 2011). This detailed work on U.S. trade treaties must have given Viner further insight into the effects of trade preferences and the political process surrounding them. Again specific examples found their way into Viner's later work, such as the U.S.-Hawaii-Cuba sugar trade (Viner 1931b, p. 7, and 1950, pp. 122–3 [96–97]).

Early Papers on Reciprocity and the Most-Favored-Nation Principle

After leaving the Tariff Commission and establishing himself in his new position at the University of Chicago, Viner began to write on these issues. An article on preferences in U.S. trade agreements (Viner 1924b) was followed by another covering similar ground in a Swedish journal (Viner 1931b). In these articles Viner showed himself a fierce defender of the MFN principle, and not overly concerned about customs unions, which he saw as an unimportant and perhaps justified exception to the principle.

Aspects of the international situation in the 1920s may have influenced Viner's approach to the economics of discriminatory trade arrangements. Following World War I and the 1916 Allied Economic Conference in Paris, some European nations were reluctant to extend MFN to Germany, reversing their pre–World War I practice. The United States was the strongest supporter of the MFN principle and in 1922 moved to unconditional acceptance of the principle (discussed in Irwin 1993). Further post–World War I European threats to the principle perhaps inclined Viner to search harder for economic arguments against discrimination to place his country's position on a firmer footing. The Tariff Commission work and the Paris conference are mentioned in Viner's early articles, and in the 1931 article he is explicit about his motivation, stating that since the MFN principle is "definitely on the defensive" it is time "to examine the objections which have been made" against "equality of treatment in tariff matters" (Viner 1931, p. 96).

Many of the ideas, and even the language, of *The Customs Union Issue* can be found in the early 1924 and 1931 articles. The concept of trade diversion and the harm done by trade-diverting agreements are clearly explained. He wrote that for the country and the world as a whole "reciprocity treaties, even on free-trade grounds, are ordinarily not an amelioration, but on the contrary are an intensification of the evils of customs tariffs. They not only do not counteract the tendency of protective import duties to divert international trade from the channels which it would follow under free trade, but they may cause an even wider departure of trade from its natural channels than would result from a regime of uniform protective tariffs at the levels prevalent prior to the grant of partial reductions of duties through reciprocity arrangements" (Viner 1924b, p. 107).

The idea of trade diversion becomes more concrete in his article for the Swedish journal on the most-favored-nation principle:

A tariff that is high, but uniform in its treatment of imports regardless of their origin, may divert trade from the channels which it would follow if allowed freely to choose its own path much less than would a moderate tariff which applies different treatment to imports according to their country of origin. Suppose that under free trade country A would find it to its advantage to import a particular commodity from

country B, and that even with a high duty it is still not possible to produce a commodity at home at a profit to its producers, so that it continues to be imported from B. While
the tariff reduces the volume of trade, it does so only as a
revenue measure, and still permits the commodity to be produced there where it can be produced most cheaply. Suppose,
now, that the duty is reduced by half on imports from a third
country, C, and that by virtue of this preferential treatment
C can undersell B and capture A's trade. The result of the
discrimination in favour of C is that the commodity which
could be most cheaply produced in B, and would be produced
there even if A had a high tariff, provided it was nondis-
criminatory, is now produced in C, where the conditions for
its production are comparatively unfavourable. The reduction in duty, because it is discriminatory and not uniformly
extended to all, operates as a deterrent instead of a stimulus
to the optimum allocation of the world's resources in production. (Viner 1931b, p. 5).

Though he later noted (Viner 1950, p. 66 [53]) that his questioning in print of customs unions began with the article in the Swedish
journal, overall he still viewed customs unions favorably: "as a rule,
customs unions probably constitute a forward step towards freer
trade" (Viner 1931, p. 10).

Manitoba Consulting Assignment

Viner's thinking on customs unions developed further through
consulting work in the late 1930s for the Province of Manitoba as
part of the Canadian Royal Commission on Dominion-Provincial
Relations. Manitoba's argument about the detrimental impact
of the Canadian Federation was explicitly framed in customs
union terms.

For our purposes Viner's (1938) supplementary statement to the Royal Commission is of most interest.[9] There he explained Manitoba's problem was that the Canadian federal tariff priced lower-cost U.S. producers out of the market, so that goods were instead imported from higher-cost Canadian producers, mostly located in Ontario. This diversion of trade affected consumer goods and inputs to Manitoba's agricultural export industries, as well as government purchases. There was little possibility of expansion of the Manitoban export industries as a result of the Canadian tariff, but large benefits to Ontario producers. The federal tariff diverted trade from the U.S. states adjacent to Manitoba despite lower transport costs than for trade with Ontario. Viner noted that while terms-of-trade benefits might also be expected as the tariff would reduce demand for imports, the fact that the foreign demand for Manitoba's exports was almost perfectly elastic meant that any terms-of-trade benefit to Manitoba would be minimal, and most of the terms-of-trade benefit would accrue to Ontario and other Canadian industrial provinces. The case of Manitoba in the Canadian Federation was a clear example of losses due to trade diversion that Viner was later to discuss in *The Customs Union Issue*.[10]

The Manitoba work was significant not for any conceptual innovation, but because it provided Viner with a concrete example that guided his thinking about the circumstances in which a

9. Viner's work with the Manitoba government is discussed in more detail in Oslington (2012). The Royal Commission on Dominion-Provincial Relations was established in 1937 by the Canadian government to examine "the economic and financial basis of Confederation and the distribution of legislative powers in the light of the economic and social developments of the last 70 years." Viner was engaged as a consultant to assist with Manitoba's submissions to the commission, and his important 1938 supplementary statement is part of the Jacob Viner Papers at Princeton.

10. Both the Manitoba and the analogous situation of Western Australian in the Australian Federation are discussed in Viner 1950, p. 86 and 127 [69 and 101].

customs union would lead to losses, and a case where the losses appeared to be substantial.

The Postwar Context: Redesigning International Trade and Financial Systems

Viner was heavily involved in the difficult discussions of the post–World War II trade and financial architecture, directly and through his extensive networks of friends and correspondents on both sides of the Atlantic, and through his writings (such as Viner 1946; 1947).[11] Advocates of free trade struggled with a system clogged by the residues of interwar protectionist measures, wartime controls, and macroeconomic imbalances. Intellectually, free traders were on the defensive. Nondiscrimination, though, was in favor in the United States after the 1934 Reciprocal Trade Agreement Act and had the support of Roosevelt's secretary of state, Cordell Hull. Viner through his advisory work for the U.S. Treasury and State Department was a key player in U.S. policy.[12]

European discussions of some form of union were encouraged by the United States to facilitate post–World War II reconstruction and to act as a bulwark against the Soviet bloc, though the 1957 Treaty of Rome, which led eventually to the European Union, was still a long way off.

The beginning of the postwar multilateralism was signaled by the 1947 Havana Charter for the proposed International Trade Organization. Customs unions, along with free trade areas, were treated in the Havana Charter as exceptions to the general

11. Further discussion of postwar trade negotiations may be found in Irwin, Mavroidis, and Sykes (2008).

12. Viner's advisory work for the U.S. Treasury and State Department, including his role in Bretton Woods, is discussed in a 1953 interview conducted as part of the Columbia Oral History Project, and Nerozzi (2011).

principle of nondiscrimination, and both were defined somewhat vaguely.[13] Although the Havana Charter was abandoned by the United States in 1950, and then died, it did entrench these MFN exceptions in subsequent General Agreement on Tariffs and Trade and World Trade Organization agreements. The relationship between customs unions and the embryonic multilateral process was then quite unclear to contemporary observers, including Viner.

A further dimension of the post–World War II debate over free trade was macroeconomic and exchange rate problems, especially the problem of dollar shortage. Viner was particularly concerned in these debates to keep the focus on the long game of free trade and resisted compromising free trade through imperfect solutions to these temporary problems (see especially Viner 1950, p. 169 [134]).[14]

Stimulus from Other International Economists

Viner's papers indicate extensive discussion of preferential trade issues with other international economists. In *The Customs Union Issue* (Viner 1950, pp. 65–66 [53–54]) he particularly notes the work of his close friend Lionel Robbins (1937, pp. 120–23), who criticized "tariff unions" as economically detrimental, writing that "The only completely innocuous tariff union would be directed against the inaccessible produce of the moon."

Gottfried Haberler (with whom Viner had clashed in the 1930s over the question of real costs versus opportunity costs as

13. Bhagwati (2008) includes an illuminating discussion of some of the sordid politics behind the inclusion of customs unions and free trade areas as exceptions to MFN in the Havana Charter.

14. Douglas Irwin's work emphasizes the connection between macroeconomic and exchange rate issues and trade policy, for instance Irwin (1993), and Irwin (2010) for the 1930s.

a basis for judgments about the gains from international trade)[15] is singled out as an example of the common position that customs unions advance the cause of free trade, and are therefore a good thing. The relevant sections of Haberler (1936, pp. 377–91) criticize "preferential duties," but "customs unions are to be wholeheartedly welcomed" (Haberler 1936, p. 390). The only way of making sense of Haberler's position is seeing him as understandably swayed by European political considerations in the 1930s rather than offering an economic argument for customs unions. His later essay (Haberler 1943) expresses support for regional trade blocs, for political as much as economic reasons.

Viner's combative nature and the opportunity of refuting a conventional view supported by prominent international economists perhaps contributed to his decision to write *the Customs Union Issue*. The overriding reason, though, was his concern for the cause of free trade, in particular the fear that the formation of customs unions would be a distraction for free traders, and an opportunity for others to disguise protectionism. As he explained in the opening pages of the book, "Projects for customs unions and other special tariff arrangements between states independent of each other politically are today widespread, and many persons look to them as at least a partial solution for the major economic and political problems in the international field" (Viner 1950, p. 1 [3]).

Writing of *The Customs Union Issue*

The book resulted from an invitation in 1944 from George Finch, a director of the Carnegie Endowment for International Peace in Washington, to write a historical and analytical essay to serve as

---

15. The real cost versus opportunity cost controversy is discussed in Oslington (2009).

an introduction "to a planned collection of customs union documents" (Finch to Viner, May 16, 1944). Viner accepted the invitation and completed the manuscript by 1948 (Viner to Finch, August 24, 1948). However, the accompanying volume of documents was abandoned by Carnegie, much to Viner's regret (Viner to Finch, October 26, 1948). A compromise was reached whereby a list of approximately 250 documents held by the Carnegie Endowment would be included as an appendix to Viner's essay. Viner's frustration grew with delays in publishing until he wrote, "I am simply disgusted" and "I wish to God that I had never started on this venture with the Carnegie Endowment" (Viner to Joseph Shotwell, April 26, 1950).

I turn now to what exactly Viner wrote (and didn't write), about which there has been much misunderstanding in the literature.

Viner took a broad view of customs unions, and his analysis is relevant to most preferential trading arrangements. The introductory chapter discusses customs unions as "one of a number of possible types of arrangement which eliminate or reduce the tariff barriers between two or more political units while maintaining tariff barriers against imports from outside regions" (p. 2 [4]), while a "perfect customs union" (p. 2 [5]) is defined as an arrangement that meets "the following conditions":

> the complete elimination of tariffs as between the member territories; the establishment of a uniform tariff on imports from outside the union; apportionment of customs revenue between the members in accordance with an agreed formula.

The economic analysis begins with Viner noting the "strange phenomenon" of support for customs unions uniting free traders and protectionists (p. 51 [41]). Their views on trade issues are generally opposite, so their unity on the customs unions issue must come from misunderstanding about whether customs unions represent a move towards free trade or away from free trade. He explains that his questions will be the effect of the customs union on each country separately, on the countries together, and the world as a whole (p. 53 [42]).

Before launching into the analysis Viner points out that "None of these questions can be answered *a priori,* and the correct answers will depend on just how the customs union operates in practice. All that *a priori* analysis can do, is to demonstrate, within limits, how the customs union must operate if it is to have specific types of consequence" (p. 53 [43]).

He then makes the crucial distinction between, on the one hand, commodities "which one of the members of the customs union will now newly import from the other but which it formerly did not import at all because the price of the protected domestic product was lower than the price at any foreign source plus the duty," that is, commodities that involve "a shift from a high-cost to a lower-cost point, a shift which the free trader can properly approve, as at least a step in the right direction, even if universal free trade would divert production to a source with still lower costs" (p. 53 [43]) and, on the other hand, "other commodities which one of the members of the customs union will now newly import from the other whereas before the customs union it imported them from a third country, because that was the cheapest possible source of supply even after payment of duty," that is, which involve a shift between "a low-cost third country and the other, high-cost, member country" (p. 53 [43]). This is the trade diversion case, and he comments that it "is a shift of the type which the protectionist approves, but it is not one which the free-trader who understands the logic of his own doctrine can properly approve" (p. 53 [43]).

The reader should always bear in mind that Viner had been commissioned to write a brief essay introducing a collection of customs union documents aimed at policymakers. He is not engaging in a detailed exercise in welfare economics; instead he is making a simple distinction that he believes will be helpful in evaluating customs unions. This approach is consistent with his other writings, where he resists elaborate theoretical systems and derived propositions that purport to settle real-world policy questions.

Reading the Viner passage as some sort of general proposition ignores the comments that precede and follow it about the impossibility of answering questions about the impact of customs unions a priori. As he emphasizes, "From the free-trade point of view, whether a particular customs union is a move in the right or in the wrong direction depends, therefore, so far as the argument has as yet been carried, on which of the two types of consequences ensue from that customs union" (p. 55 [44]).

If Viner offers welfare propositions anywhere, it is not on pages 53–55 [43–44], but at the end of his brief discussion of the economics of customs unions, where he gives several rules of thumb:

A customs union is more likely to operate in the free-trade direction, whether appraisal is in terms of its consequences for the customs union area alone or for the world as a whole:

(1) the larger the economic area of the customs union and therefore the greater the potential scope for internal division of labor;
(2) the lower the "average" tariff level on imports from outside the customs union area as compared to what the level would be in the absence of customs union;
(3) the greater the correspondence in kind of products of the range of high-cost industries as between the different parts of the customs union which were protected by tariffs in both of the member countries before the customs union was established i.e., the *less* the degree of

complementarity—or the *greater* the degree of rivalry—
of the member countries with respect to *protected* industries, prior to the customs union;

(4) the greater the differences in unit-costs for protected
industries of the same kind as between the different
parts of the customs union, and therefore the greater the
economies to be derived from free trade with respect to
these industries within the customs union area;

(5) the higher the tariff levels in potential export markets
outside the customs union area with respect to commodities in whose production the member countries
of the customs union would have a comparative advantage under free trade, and therefore the less the injury
resulting from reducing the degree of specialization in
production as between the customs union area and the
outside world;

(6) the greater the range of protected industries for which
an enlargement of the market would result in unit-costs
lower than those at which the commodities concerned
could be imported from outside the customs union area;

(7) the smaller the range of protected industries for which an
enlargement of the market would not result in unit-costs
lower than those at which the commodities concerned
could be imported from outside the customs union area
but which would nevertheless expand under customs
union. (p. 63–4 [51])

As was Viner's habit, he follows a simple and suggestive piece of
economic theory with a list of qualifications and additional matters
which need to be considered by policymakers. Here the additional
matters are the possibility of a customs union being able to exploit
market power and improve its terms of trade (bringing gains at the
expense of the outside world) (p. 69 [55]), better possibilities of

bargaining for tariff reductions (p. 69 [56]), administrative economies flowing from customs unions (pp. 73–77 [58–64]), revenue from duties (pp. 81–82 [65–68]), and the impact of forming a customs union on the degree of monopoly within the union (pp. 94–97 [75–78]).

Viner showed a keen awareness of the political dimensions of customs unions. An important question was the relationship between economic union and political union, because some economists advanced customs unions as a step toward political unions that would help secure a lasting peace. Viner argued historically that most customs unions that had actually been formed were driven by political rather than economic considerations (p. 115 [91]), that political union always preceded economic union for good reasons (such as the absence of workable redistributive mechanisms). Moreover the most economically beneficial customs unions are the hardest to form (p. 171 [135]), a point rediscovered by Grossman and Helpman (1995) and the contemporary political economy of customs union literature.

A comment on this "strange phenomenon" of customs unions pleasing both free traders and protectionists shows his awareness of the political economy issues. He suggests that "Businessmen...and governments which have had to try to simultaneously satisfy both special interests seeking increased protection and voters hostile to protection have long known ways of making increased protection look like movement in a free-trade direction" (p. 59 [48]), then gives an example of another way protectionism can be made to look like free-trade policy. This is when reducing a duty on an input (woolen cloth) increases protection overall (on woolen goods), a situation that would later be considered by the effective protection literature (Corden 1971).

Viner also offers perceptive commentary on the relationship between customs unions and the multilateral trade liberalization process that was beginning to take shape as he wrote. He feared that in the postwar period customs unions would "almost inevitably operate as a psychological barrier to the realization of the more desirable but less desired objectives of the Havana Charter—the balanced multilateral reduction of trade barriers on a non-discriminatory basis" (p. 176 [139]), and this has sadly proved true, as discussed by Bhagwati (2008) and others.

These sorts of political considerations are at least as important as the economic arguments about trade diversion to his conclusion that "customs union is only a partial, uncertain, and otherwise imperfect means of doing what world-wide non-discriminatory reduction of trade barriers can do more fully, more certainly, and more equitably" (p. 170 [135]).

Reception of Viner's Work

Early Reviews

Sales of *The Customs Union Issue* were healthy, and reviews in economics, political science, and history journals were universally positive.[16] Most praised Viner for his command of the historical material and commented on the relevance of the book for current controversies.

A few reviews by economists highlighted analytical contributions. Virgil Salera (1951, p. 84) in the *Journal of Political Economy* considered it "the first rigorous treatment of the subject" and focused on how Viner's trade diversion argument overturned the conventional wisdom that customs unions were always a good

---

16. The book sold well at $2.50 (Correspondence, October 18, 1950) and Viner was paid an honorarium of $500. The Carnegie endowment gave Anderson Kramer Associates of Washington, DC, permission to reprint the book in 1961, but it has been out of print since that time. It is now quite rare on the secondhand book market, and prices on a sample of bookseller websites range from about $80 to $450. So far it seems to have escaped the Google Books scanners.

thing. Wolfgang Stolper described the book in his review for the *American Economic Review* as "the most cogent analysis of the economics of customs unions to be found in the literature. But this means perhaps only that the book was written by Jacob Viner" (Stolper 1951, p. 990). He correctly identified Viner's main concern as sorting out whether customs unions contributed to the cause of free trade, and understanding why customs unions might be supported by protectionists for trade diversion or cartelization reasons. James Meade's review for *Economica* praised it highly: "A good book on the subject of the customs union has for long been wanted; and now it is provided by Professor Viner's study, which it is difficult to praise too highly" (Meade 1951, p. 186). He predicted that "Professor Viner's study on the economic aspects of customs unions will be of central interest to economists. Indeed for many years this is likely to remain the locus classicus for the economic analysis of customs-union problems" (Meade 1951, p. 187). There is an exposition of Viner's argument about trade diversion and creation, but no comments on Viner's assumptions or their limitations.

Meade

James Meade was the first economist to further develop Viner's insights in a series of invited lectures in Rotterdam (Meade 1955). The admiring comments from the review are repeated, but he also observes "like many basic ideas which have broken new ground and suggested the lines of work, his analysis is in my opinion in some respects incomplete; and when an attempt is made complete it, it no longer remains as simple in its application as may at first sight appear to be the case. It is my purpose in these lectures to make a contribution to the analysis which Professor Viner has started" (p. 34). Meade's criticism is that "Professor Viner's analysis does not tell one how to weigh up the economic gains from some element of trade creation against the economic losses from some other elements of trade diversion" (p. 34). In order to do this Meade sets out a model where "all elasticities of demand are zero, and all elasticities of supply are infinite." In the chapters that follow this model is analyzed and extended in various ways, and Meade concludes that "it is impossible to pass judgment upon customs unions in general" (p. 107). There is no denying the richness of Meade's discussion and the acute powers of insight demonstrated, especially in the "rash generalizations" he gives at the end of the lectures (pp. 117–24).

Meade claims when developing his model that it is "completely in harmony" (p. 36) with Viner's; however, later in the book there are statements without clear textual support that Viner assumes "constant costs of production" and "zero elasticities of demand" (Meade 1955, p. 77). While nothing Meade writes directly contradicts statements by Viner, he is using Viner's work as an anchor for his own development of customs union theory.

Lipsey

Richard Lipsey was at the time undertaking a PhD at the London School of Economics on customs unions (his thesis was subsequently published as Lipsey 1970), and marks of Meade's reading of Viner are evident in an article Lipsey (1957) published in *Economica*. This article takes Viner's comment about a free trader properly approving of trade creation, but not trade diversion (see Viner 1950, p. 43), as a formal proposition of welfare economics and proceeds to demolish it as such. In a competitive general equilibrium model consumption effects can work in the direction opposite to those that Lipsey sees as emerging from Viner's problematic analysis of the production side. A similar position is taken in his survey Lipsey (1960), although the statement about Viner's assumptions is softened slightly to "Viner's analysis implicitly assumed that commodities are consumed in some fixed proportion which is independent of the structure of relative prices" (p. 499).

Lipsey suggests his analysis is more general and therefore superior; and that Viner's insights on customs unions are merely a special case of his general theorem of second best (Lipsey and Lancaster 1956). Conceptually Lipsey is right that the economics of customs unions is a special case of the theory of second-best, but historically the theory of second best is an outgrowth of customs union theory and other areas of economics such as public finance. The importance of customs unions for the development of the general theory is suggested by Meade's work on customs unions leading to his own independent statement of the theory of second best in his classic *Trade and Welfare* (Meade 1956). Viner's work on customs unions clearly influenced Lipsey, as he acknowledges in the discussion of precursors of the theory of second best (Lipsey and Lancaster 1956, pp. 13–14). There are statements of what looks like a generalized theory of second-best in Viner's work (for example, the introduction to Viner 1951, p. 12), but Viner had no interest in pressing claims.[17]

Corden

Max Corden's (1965) fine survey of developments in international trade theory unfortunately relied too much on Meade's

17. Viner never pressed his justified claims to priority here or elsewhere. The vanity of hunting for precursors of current theories was frequently pointed out by Viner, and he avoided it in his own historical work. Instead he gives a rule (Viner 1937, p. 442) that he used to adjudicate Ricardo and Torrens' claims in relation to comparative advantage. Viner writes that Ricardo "is entitled to the credit for first giving due emphasis to the doctrine, for first placing it in an appropriate setting, and for obtaining general acceptance of it by economists" (p. 442). Under this Viner rule Lipsey and Lancaster would be entitled to credit for the theory of second best, and Viner seems happy to allow this.

and Lipsey's accounts of Viner's work on customs unions. His opening statement, "The theory of customs unions is a completely new branch of the theory of tariffs. It originated with Viner's *The Customs Union Issue* 1950. Since 1955 it has been rapidly elaborated by Meade, Lipsey, and others, who have shown that it is one of the most important applications of the theory of second-best" (p. 52), is open to question on a number of grounds. He also claims "Viner has ignored the consumption affects, and assumed that commodities were consumed in fixed proportions, unaffected by changes in relative prices brought about by the customs union" (p. 52), though Corden praises Viner's work overall.

Cordon's reception of Viner is illuminated by subsequent correspondence between Corden and Viner.[18] This correspondence with Max Corden is one of the few times Viner commented on his work on customs unions. Viner was provoked to write after reading Corden's survey, "I must say that I found some difficulty in recognizing the relevance to what I published in 1950 of some of what you attribute to me with respect to customs unions." Viner especially objected to the assertion that he assumed "that commodities were consumed in fixed proportions unaffected by the changes in relative prices brought about by the customs union." He adds, "if this is nevertheless a necessary implication of something I did say, I would regard it as a monstrous lapse on my part, but would ask where precisely I was guilty of this lapse."

Viner also objects to Corden's charge that he "assumed constant costs," believing he "had been sufficiently explicit on my pages 45 and 47 [56 and 58]," and states that he worked with "increasing cost as the one generally prevailing (static) pattern of costs relative to output." On this he adds, "if there is even the slightest

18. This letter from Viner on March 13, 1965, was made available by Max Corden and published in the *Journal of International Economics* 6(1) (1976): 107–8. Viner's copy of the letter is among his papers held by the Mudd Manuscript Library at Princeton.

implication in anything I wrote in the customs union issue of an assumption of constant costs, I would certainly like to have it identified, so that I could engage in what I would regard as due penance." The point is reinforced by a reference to increasing costs in his famous article on cost and supply curves Viner (1931a). Some confusion seems to exist over whether constant costs refers to diminishing returns or constant returns to scale. Viner concludes the letter, "I have so much respect for the superior competence in analytical matters of the present generation of economists that I am ready humbly to accept their verdicts... provided only that they base their verdicts on what I have actually written." Corden wrote back quickly: "I assume that I was in error, since you will know best what you wrote and what your intentions were. It seems to me possible that I may have been (over) influenced in my interpretation by Lipsey's writings" (Corden to Viner, April 5, 1965).

Later Corden (1972) developed the theory of customs unions with nonconstant returns to scale, remedying the defect in Viner. He acknowledges Viner's discussion (1950, pp. 56–59 [45–47]) of increasing returns to scale as an argument for customs unions and comments that some of his conclusions differ from Viner's "possibly because his (unspecified) assumptions differ" (Corden 1972, p. 465). In the end, though, Corden reaffirms Viner's suggestion that increasing returns do not greatly affect the analysis of customs unions.

Cooper and Massell

The point of departure for Cooper and Massell's (1965) supposedly new view of customs unions was Viner's statement that nations had no incentive to form customs unions because any benefit from a customs union could be more efficiently obtained from trade liberalization on an MFN basis (Viner 1950, p. 170 [135]). Viner had made exactly the same argument in his earliest paper on the subject: "In so far as the advantages derivable from such [reciprocity] arrangements are economic, however, they are obtainable in at least equal degree through the outright reduction of their tariffs by both countries" (Viner 1924, p. 108).

Krauss

Melvyn Krauss's landmark (1972) *Journal of Economic Literature* survey entrenched Meade's, Lipsey's, and Corden's readings of Viner's work, though he lauded Viner as the pioneer of customs unions theory and developer of the concepts of trade creation and diversion. Krauss saw the subsequent literature as a response to the limitations of Viner's analysis—saying in particular that it was "based on the number of simplifying assumptions—fixed proportions in consumption and constant costs" in production (Krauss 1972, p. 414).

Michaely

Michael Michaely's (1976) *Journal of International Economics* paper was the last detailed practitioner engagement with Viner's work, with a title promising a resolution of the disputed question of Viner's assumptions. He begins with the fair comment that "Viner's discussion is expressed in a rather intuitive manner, lacking a precise specification of the analytical model and its basic assumptions. Consequently, possible misinterpretations of Viner's position have been accepted as conventional wisdom" (Michaely 1976, p. 75). But then follows a common but dubious historical procedure of building a convenient model and trying to squeeze the writer in question into it. Michaely's model (pp. 75–82) is a standard small open economy general equilibrium model with given factor endowments and appropriate assumptions about technology to generate a convex production transformation frontier. He examines key passages of Viner's book with the aid of this reference model, and finds Viner's analysis wanting. Within the framework of his reference model Michaely is forced to conclude that Viner has made some very strange and contradictory assumptions, for instance ignoring substitution in consumption. However, the problem seems to be more with the attempt to impose a simplified model on Viner's rich but admittedly vague analysis. Examination of Viner's more formal modeling work should have suggested to Michaely that Viner could not plausibly be accused of ignoring substitution in consumption. Michaely in my view was unsuccessful in resolving the question of Viner's assumptions. Viner obviously had a model or models in mind when describing the effects of customs unions, but it is unclear exactly what they were.

Viner's lack of clarity about his assumptions is due partly to the nature of the book and partly his skepticism of the sort of exercises of which Michaely's paper is an example. The approach is perfectly consistent with views he expressed elsewhere on modeling. For instance, Viner (1937, p. 526) suggested it is appropriate to leave analysis "in that state of persuasiveness associated with incomplete demonstration which seems to be a universal characteristic of propositions economic theory relating to questions involving human welfare." Or consider Viner (1955, p. 128), where he suggested "relevance is of supreme importance for economic theory" and "leads to certain rules of guidance as to the procedure we should follow in constructing our theoretical models," including "the practice to start with the simplest and the most rigorous model, and to leave it to a later stage, or to others, to introduce into the model additional variables or other complicating elements." He is scathing in other writings about taking propositions deduced from models directly to policy discussion.

Contemporary Consensus

Viner's *Customs Union Issue* is no longer much read by practitioners, nor does it directly stimulate theoretical development in the way it did through the 1950s and 1960s. It would no longer be possible to publish an article in a major economics journal by pointing out a shortcoming in Viner's work, as many did in the 1950s and 1960s. Among practitioners, Viner's work is considered to have been fully mined and its interpretation settled. This is clear in the recent surveys of the economics of customs unions or preferential trading arrangements, which usually open with a mention of Viner's book and his contribution to the field but seldom engage with the text in any depth, and even clearer if one opens a sample of current major journal papers on preferential trading arrangements.[19]

Instead the book now functions as a classic,[20] where prominent reference to *The Customs Union Issue* identifies a contemporary work as belonging to the literature on preferential trading arrangements within the subdiscipline of economics. Besides being an emblem—almost a badge of membership for a particular group of economists—the other function of a classic is as an authority. Citing Viner's position on an issue has some rhetorical

19. Recent surveys include Bhagwati (1993, 2008), who picks up Viner's argument that the formation of customs unions is something fundamentally different from free trade, but neglects parts of Viner's book that connect with his own discussion of dynamic and political economy aspects of customs unions; Krishna (2008), for whom Viner is the pioneer of the static welfare analysis of customs unions; and Freund and Ornelas (2010), who identify Viner as the originator of the distinction between trade diversion and trade creation, and this distinction gives their survey shape as they assess whether recent empirical and political economy studies indicate whether trade diversion or creation predominates.

20. The meaning of a classic is discussed in Oslington (2013) using Viner's work as an example. There seems to be a reading cycle where a work recognized as being of value is used by practitioners, and may then become a classic which functions as emblem and authority. Later it may become an object of historical study.

force, but less force now among economists than in some of the other disciplines Viner addressed.

Assessment of Viner's Contribution

Viner wrote *The Customs Union Issue* because he valued the benefits of free trade, and at a deeper level the liberal economic order. His purpose was to disturb the common view among economists and policymakers that a customs union must be a move in the direction of free trade. Part of the strategy involved a simple informally expressed model of trade creation and diversion, but this model by no means exhausts the factors to be considered when assessing customs unions. Economies of scale, effects on the degree of competition, and impact on the politics of the multilateral trade liberalization process also matter greatly. As he emphasized, the effects of customs unions cannot be determined theoretically, and a policymaker must carefully consider the particular circumstances of any proposed customs union. Considering the history, Viner succeeded admirably in his purpose.

However, assessing a work in relation to its author's purpose, in its original context, is not the same as assessing its enduring significance. What if anything can contemporary international economists and policymakers take from *The Customs Union Issue*? I would suggest several things.

First, the analysis of preferential trading arrangements needs to be kept close to Viner's fundamental question of whether the arrangement promotes or hinders free trade. This was also the fundamental question of the classical economists. After more than fifty years of work on the economics of preferential trading arrangements, there is a need to reintegrate it with the core of international economics. It is not some exotic optional extra but belongs as part of the core.

Second, we can learn from Viner that there are macroeconomic and exchange rate dimensions to preferential trade issues. They have perhaps not received the attention they deserve here, but the work of Douglas Irwin and others shows how the barter trade and monetary considerations interact and how a stable macroeconomic environment assists trade liberalization

Third, politics matters. Viner integrated political considerations into his economic analysis in a way that can be developed with the more powerful economics of politics tools that contemporary international economists have at their disposal, for instance, in the recent work of Grossman and Helpman, and Jagdish Bhagwati.

Editorial Policy for This Volume

This volume reproduces Viner's original 1950 text in full, omitting only the list of customs union documents and the portion of the bibliography associated with that list. Pagination of the original is indicated by page numbers that appear in square brackets near the cross references of the original. The index is Viner's, modified for the above omissions. I have resisted the temptation to remove passages and footnotes that appear to have limited enduring significance. As has been emphasized in the introduction, Viner is not attempting a timeless and contextless statement of the economics of customs unions. He is working in a particular situation with particular influences, and keeping these passages reinforces that message. Removing such passages would also remove rich illustrative material on which the arguments draw.

References

Baldwin, Richard E., and A. J. Venables (1995). "Regional Economic Integration." In *Handbook of International Economics,* volume 3, edited by G. M. Grossman and K. Rogoff. Amsterdam: North-Holland. 1597–1644.

Baumol, William J., and Ellen Viner-Seiler (1979). "Jacob Viner." In *International Encyclopedia of the Social Sciences,* volume 18, *Biographical Supplement,* edited by D. Sills. New York: Free Press.

Bhagwati, Jagdish (1993). "Multilateralism and Regionalism: An Overview." In *New Dimensions in Regional Integration*, edited by J. De Melo and A. Panagariya. Cambridge: Cambridge University Press.

Bhagwati, Jagdish (2008). *Termites in the Trading System: How Preferential Agreements Undermine Free Trade.* New York: Oxford University Press.

Bhagwati, Jagdish, and Arvind Panagariya (1996). "Theory of Preferential Trade Agreements: Historical Evolution and Current Trends." *American Economic Review* 86(2): 82–87.

Blaug, Mark (1991). *Great Economists after Keynes.* London: Harvester Wheatsheaf.

Bloomfield, Arthur I. (1992). "On the Centenary of Jacob Viner's Birth: A Retrospective View of the Man and His Work." *Journal of Economic Literature* 30(4): 2052–85.

Cooper, C. A., and B. F. Massell (1965). "A New Look at Customs Union Theory." *Economic Journal* 75(300): 742–77.

Corden, W. Max (1965). *Recent Developments in the Theory of International Trade.* Princeton, NJ: International Finance Section.

Corden, W. Max (1971). *The Theory of Protection.* Oxford: Clarendon.

Corden, W. Max (1972). "Economies of Scale and Customs Union Theory." *Journal of Political Economy* 80(3): 465–75.

Freund, Caroline, and Emanuel Ornelas (2010). "Regional Trade Agreements." *Annual Review of Economics* 2: 139–66.

Groenewegen, Peter D. (1994). "Jacob Viner and the History of Economic Thought." *Contributions to Political Economy* 13: 69–86.

Grossman, Gene M., and Elhanan Helpman (1994). "Protection for Sale." *American Economic Review* 84(4): 833–50.

Grossman, Gene M., and Elhanan Helpman (1995). "The Politics of Free-Trade Agreements." *American Economic Review* 85(4): 667–90.

Haberler, Gottfried (1936). *The Theory of International Trade with Its Applications to Commercial Policy*. London: William Hodge.

Haberler, Gottfried (1943). "The Political Economy of Regional or Continental Blocs." In *Postwar Economic Problems*, edited by Seymour E. Harris. New York: McGraw-Hill. 325–44.

Irwin, Douglas A. (1991). Introduction to *Jacob Viner: Essays on the Intellectual History of Economics*. Princeton: Princeton University Press.

Irwin, Douglas A. (1993). "Multilateral and Bilateral Trade Policies in the World Trading System: An Historical Perspective." In *New Dimensions in Regional Integration*, edited by J. De Melo and A. Panagariya. Cambridge: Cambridge University Press. pp. 90–118.

Irwin, Douglas A. (2011). *Peddling Protectionism: Smoot-Hawley and the Great Depression*. Princeton: Princeton University Press.

Irwin, Douglas A., Petros C. Mavroidis, and A. O. Sykes (2008). *The Genesis of the GATT*. New York: Cambridge University Press.

Krishna, Pravin (2008). "Regional and Preferential Trade Agreements." In *New Palgrave Dictionary of Economics,* edited by Steven N. Durlaf and Lawrence E. Blume. 2nd edition. London: Palgrave Macmillan.

Krauss, M. B. (1972). "Recent Developments in Customs Union Theory: An Interpretive Survey." *Journal of Economic Literature* 10(2): 413–36.

Lipsey, Richard G. (1957). "The Theory of Customs Unions: Trade Diversion and Welfare." *Economica, n.s.* 24(93): 40–46.

Lipsey, Richard G. (1960). "The Theory of Customs Unions: A General Survey." *Economic Journal* 70(279): 496–513.

Lipsey, Richard G. (1970). *The Theory of Customs Unions: A General Equilibrium Analysis*. London: Weidenfeld and Nicolson.

Lipsey, Richard G., and Kelvin Lancaster (1956). "The General Theory of Second Best." *Review of Economic Studies* 24(1): 11–32.

Lloyd, P. J., and D. Maclaren (2004). "Gains and Losses from Regional Trading Arrangements: A Survey." *Economic Record* 80(251): 445–67.

Meade, J. E. (1951). "The Removal of Trade Barriers: The Regional Versus the Universal Approach." *Economica* 18(70): 184–98.

Meade, J. E. (1955). *The Theory of Customs Unions*. Amsterdam: North Holland.

Meade, J. E. (1956). *Trade and Welfare (with Mathematical Supplement)*. Oxford: Oxford University Press.

Meardon, Stephen (2011). "On the Evolution of U.S. Trade Agreements: Evidence from Taussig's Tariff Commission." *Journal of Economic Issues* 45(2): 475–83.

Michaely, Michael (1976). "The Assumptions of Jacob Viner's Theory of Customs Unions." *Journal of International Economics* 6(1): 75–93.

Nerozzi, S. (2011). "From the Great Depression to Bretton Woods: Jacob Viner and International Monetary Stabilization." *European Journal for the History of European Thought* 18(1): 55–84.

O'Brien, Denis P. (1976). "Customs Unions: Trade Creation and Trade Diversion in Historical Perspective." *History of Political Economy* 8(4): 540–63.

O'Brien, Denis P. (2004). *The Classical Economists Revisited.* Princeton: Princeton University Press.

Oslington, Paul (2008). "Jacob Viner on Religion and Intellectual History." Paper presented at History of Economics Society Conference, Washington, DC, July.

Oslington, Paul (2009). "Jacob Viner, Bertil Ohlin and Gottfried Haberler on Real vs Opportunity Cost: Clash of the Titans, Sterile Controversy, or What?" Paper presented at History of Economic Thought Society of Australia Conference, Fremantle, July.

Oslington, Paul (2012). "Jacob Viner, the Cost of Protection and Customs Unions: New Light from a Manitoba Consulting Assignment." *History of Economics Review* 55 (Winter) 73–79.

Oslington, Paul (2013). "Contextual History, Practitioner History and Classic Status: Reading Jacob Viner's *The Customs Union Issue*." *Journal of the History of Economic Thought* 35(4) forthcoming.

Panagariya, Arvind (2000). "Preferential Trade Liberalization: The Traditional Theory and New Developments." *Journal of Economic Literature* 38(2): 287–331.

Pomfret, Richard (2001). *The Economics of Regional Trading Arrangements.* Oxford: Oxford University Press.

Robbins, Lionel (1937). *Economic Planning and International Order.* London: Macmillan.

Robbins, Lionel (1970). *Jacob Viner: A Tribute.* Princeton: Princeton University Press.

Salera, Virgil (1951). "Review of Jacob Viner 'The Customs Union Issue.'" *Journal of Political Economy* 59(1): 84.

Sally, Razeen (1998). *Classical Liberalism and International Economic Order: Studies in Theory and Intellectual History.* London: Routledge.

Stolper, W. (1951). "Review of Jacob Viner 'The Customs Union Issue.'" *American Economic Review* 41(5): 989–91.

Taussig, Frank W. (1892). "Reciprocity." *Quarterly Journal of Economics* 7(1): 26–39.

Taussig, Frank W. (1910). *The Tariff History of the United States.* 5th edition. New York: G.P. Putnam's Sons.

Taussig, F. W. (1915). *Some Aspects of the Tariff Question.* Cambridge, MA: Harvard University Press.

United States Tariff Commission (1919). *Reciprocity and Commercial Treaties.* Washington, DC: US Government Printing Office.

Viner, Jacob (1924a). *Canada's Balance of International Indebtedness: 1900–1913.* Cambridge, MA: Harvard University Press.

Viner, Jacob (1924b). "The Most-Favored-Nation Clause in American Commercial Treaties." *Journal of Political Economy* 32(1): 101–29. Reprinted in Viner 1951.

Viner, Jacob (1927). "Adam Smith and Laissez Faire." *Journal of Political Economy* 35(April): 198–232. Reprinted in Irwin 1991.

Viner, Jacob (1931a). "Cost Curves and Supply Curves." *Zeitschrift fur Nationalokonomie* 3: 23–46.

Viner, Jacob (1931b). "The Most-Favored-Nation Clause." *Index* 61(February): 2–17. Reprinted in Viner 1951.

Viner, Jacob (1937). *Studies in the Theory of International Trade.* London: Allen and Unwin.

Viner, Jacob (1938). "Manitoba's Argument with Respect to the Burden on the Prairie Provinces as a Result of Dominion Tariff Policy—a Supplementary Statement." Manuscript in Jacob Viner Papers.

Viner, Jacob (1946). "International Finance in the Postwar World." *Lloyds Bank Review* Reprinted in *Journal of Political Economy* 55(2) (1947): 97–107. Reprinted in Viner 1951.

Viner, Jacob (1947). "International Economic Cooperation." In *The United States in the Post-War World,* edited by William B. Willcox and Robert B. Hall. Reprinted in Viner 1951.

Viner, Jacob (1950). *The Customs Union Issue.* New York: Carnegie Endowment for International Peace.

Viner, Jacob (1951). *International Economics.* Glencoe, IL: Free Press. Collection of Viner's essays.

Viner, Jacob (1952). *International Trade and Economic Development.* Glencoe, IL: Free Press.

Viner, Jacob (1953). "Interview by Mr Wendell Link on Feb 11, 1953 at Princeton." Oral History Project, Columbia University Library. Published by L. Fiorito and S. Nerozzi as "Viner's Reminiscences from the New Deal," *Research in the History of Economic Thought and Methodology,* 27A, June 2009, 75–136.

Viner, Jacob (1955). "International Trade Theory and Its Present Day Relevance." In *Economics and Public Policy,* edited by Arthur Smithies. Washington DC, Brookings Institution. 100–130.

Vines, D. and B. Zissimos (2008). "Is the WTO's Article XXIV Bad?" Department of Economics Working Paper, University of Oxford.

Winch, Donald (1981). "Jacob Viner." *American Scholar* 50(4): 519–25.

Winch, Donald (1983). "Jacob Viner as Intellectual Historian." *Research in the History of Economic Thought and Methodology* 1: 1–17.

THE CUSTOMS
UNION ISSUE

Chapter I

Introduction

Projects for customs unions and other special tariff arrangements between states independent of each other politically are today widespread, and many persons look to them as at least a partial solution for the major economic and political problems in the international field. The United States Government has in recent years given strong support to this idea in many ways, and the Committee of European Economic Cooperation established to collaborate with the United States in the execution of the Marshall Plan for aid to Europe, no doubt in response to its interpretation of American wishes, has likewise expressed its sympathy with this idea as relates to Europe and has set up a "Study Group for the European Customs Union" to explore the possibilities.[1] The Carnegie Endowment has made a collection of texts of past customs unions consummated or officially projected, the first comprehensive collection of its kind, and on the basis of these texts and of the experience in connection with past customs unions the writer has attempted in the present study to throw some light on the possibilities and the limitations of customs unions as a method of regulating international commercial relations.

No attempt is made here to give a history either of the customs union movement in general or of any particular customs

1. See Committee of European Economic Cooperation, *General Report*, Paris, September 21, 1947 (U. S. Department of State, Publication 2930), I, 34–37.

union. Every important customs union of the past has had its historian, and several accounts of the general movement, at least up to World War I, have been published.[2] This study will, instead, examine the nature, purposes, and mode of operation of the customs union as one special form of tariff unification, primarily from the point of view of the economist. Historical material is made use of, but with no attempt at exhaustiveness, and with the sole purpose of illustrating by realistic examples or supplying evidence on the issues raised in the course of the analysis.

The customs union is only one of a number of possible types of arrangement which eliminate or reduce the tariff barriers between two or more political units while maintaining tariff barriers against imports from outside regions. Its economic difference from reciprocal free trade unaccompanied by the other criteria of customs union is slight, while, if the removal of internal trade barriers is incomplete, its legal and administrative differences from ordinary "reciprocity" agreements are also slight or questionable. The more or less "complete" or "perfect" customs union, nevertheless, acquired in the nineteenth century special importance both as fact and as project because of conditions largely peculiar to that century, as compared to earlier times. The nineteenth-century conditions which gave to the customs union a special significance have largely disappeared or are in apparent process of erosion; the nineteenth-century attitudes, however, largely survive, except that they have been transferred, together with a related transfer of nomenclature, to other types of tariff agreements which in the nineteenth century were

---

2. See especially L. Bosc, *Unions douanières et projets douanières* (Paris, 1904); Juda Pentmann, *Die Zollunionsidee und ihre Wandlungen...* (Jena, 1917). A brief account of customs union projects launched during the interwar period is given in United Nations, Department of Economic Affairs, *Customs Unions* (Lake Success, 1947), pp. 23–29; this study was prepared by the League of Nations Mission in the United States. It will hereinafter be referred to as *Customs Unions, 1947*.

more or less sharply differentiated from "customs unions." As will be explained in the following section, the historical importance of that special form of tariff agreement known as "customs union" derives largely, though not wholly, from the fact that in the nineteenth century the widespread existence of contractual obligations not to resort to tariff discrimination, and the general acceptance of customs union as a derogation from such obligations, tended to restrict the field for special tariff arrangements between independent countries to agreements of a type which could plausibly be held to meet the criteria of a "customs union."

Chapter II

The Compatibility of Customs Union with the Most-Favored-Nation Principle

1. The Criteria of a "Customs Union"

It has been generally agreed that a perfect customs union must meet the following conditions:

(1) the complete elimination of tariffs as between the member territories;

(2) the establishment of a uniform tariff on imports from outside the union;

(3) apportionment of customs revenue between the members in accordance with an agreed formula.[1]

---

1. Cf. the definition by Cavour in 1857, referred to *infra*, p. 7. Cf. also the letter of June, 1890, from Secretary of State Blaine to President Harrison transmitting a report on "Customs Union" adopted by the Inter-American Conference (51st Congress, 1st Session, Senate Executive Document No. 158, p. 2): the Conference Committee, in the words of the Secretary, interpreted "customs union" to mean "an association or agreement among the several American nations for a free interchange of domestic products, a common and uniform system of tariff laws and an equitable division of the customs dues collected under them." For full text of the Committee's Report, see International American Conference, *Reports of Committees and Discussions Thereon* (Washington, 1890), p. 103; also in *The International Conferences of American States, 1889–1928* (Carnegie Endowment for International Peace; New York, 1931), pp. 33–35.

Under the standard or "unconditional" interpretation of the most-favored-nation principle—given the absence of express agreement to limit its scope—a country, A, which is obligated by treaty to give most-favored-nation treatment to another country, B, must admit imports from B on as favorable terms as it admits similar imports from any third country, C. The question of compatibility of customs union with most-favored-nation obligations obviously arises. It is not only a question, moreover, of express contractual obligations. Long before the beginning of the nineteenth century, equality of treatment in tariff matters as between foreign countries had become a sort of general principle of international comity, to be applied to all friendly countries even in the absence of express agreement to do so unless very special circumstances could be invoked to justify departure from the principle. While a country free from legal obligations to *grant* most-favored-nation treatment could *legally* withhold it, it would also thereby put itself in a position where it could not consistently claim most-favored-nation treatment from other countries.

It came to be widely accepted, however, that the most-favored-nation obligation did not cover the commercial relations *inter se* of members of a customs union, since by virtue of such union they had become for tariff purposes, even if for no other purpose, a single entity in their relations with outside states. International lawyers have generally, though not universally, expounded this thesis.[2] Perhaps more significant than the opinions of the legal scholars was the fact that German states in the early part of the nineteenth century had set up a series of customs unions without arousing serious protest from countries outside the unions on grounds of rights to most-favored-nation treatment and without suffering in any instance the loss of

---

2. See N. Ito, *La clause de la nation la plus favorisée* (Paris, 1930), pp. 295–303, for a discussion of the legal aspects of the problem, and for citations of authorities.

most-favored-nation privileges in outside countries as a consequence of their membership in such unions.

2. Diplomatic Controversies Arising out of Most-Favored-Nation Obligations of Members of Customs Unions

The issue of compatibility of customs union with most-favored-
nation obligations did, however, on several occasions give rise to
diplomatic controversy. The issue still has significance, since it
is the question of compatibility with most-favored-nation obligations which alone makes precise and authoritative definition
of "customs union" of practical consequence and which imposes
external limitations on the specific form which shall be given to
special international tariff arrangements by the participating
countries. As no study appears ever to have been made of the
diplomatic history of the issue, an account in some detail is presented here of the diplomatic controversies which the issue has
occasioned, in so far as the writer has been able to trace them.

   In 1832, Frankfort signed a commercial treaty with England
providing for most-favored-nation treatment. As surrounding
states adhered to the Prussian Zollverein, however, Frankfort
found herself increasingly isolated economically and became willing to enter the Zollverein. In 1835, therefore, Frankfort asked
England for leave to abandon her promise of most-favored-nation
treatment, which was granted. All parties concerned seem to
have taken it for granted that in the absence of English consent
Frankfort was bound by the treaty of 1832 with England not to
enter the Zollverein.[3]

---

3. Cf. *British and Foreign State Papers,* XIX (1831–1832), 299–308; XXIII (1834–
1835), 341–43.

In 1867, when the Zollverein adopted a new constitution and took into membership some additional German states, Napoleon III claimed, on the strength of the most-favored-nation clause in the Franco-Prussian commercial treaty of 1865, the extension by Prussia to French goods of the free entry granted to Bavarian, etc., goods. The French claim was energetically denied.[4]

The issue had arisen, and in sharper form, in connection with the "customs union treaty" of 1857 between Austria and Modena (and Parma). Austria had in 1852 negotiated with Modena a customs union treaty which apparently went without protest from third countries. In 1857, Austria negotiated a revised arrangement which involved less complete tariff unification than the 1852 treaty. An Austro-Sardinian commercial treaty of 1851 provided for reciprocal most-favored-nation treatment: a separate article, however, exempted from most-favored-nation obligations the concessions made to third countries by virtue of a "complete" customs union. The Austro-Modena treaty of 1857, moreover, contained a secret clause making it inoperative if Austria could not obtain admission by the Zollverein and Sardinia that it provided for a "complete" customs union.

Cavour, on behalf of Sardinia, protested against the 1857 treaty on the ground that the tariff arrangement it provided for did not constitute a complete customs union and therefore was in violation of Austria's obligations to Sardinia. Cavour maintained that a customs union involved the fusion of the tariff interests of two or more states. If certain conditions were not met, or the greater part of them, there was only a commercial treaty and not a genuine customs union, whatever name and form may have been given to the arrangement by the contracting parties. He specified four conditions which a tariff arrangement must meet to constitute a customs union: uniformity of

4. Cf. W. O. Henderson, *The Zollverein* (Cambridge, England, 1939), p. 310.

export and transit tariffs; free exchange of the products of the united countries; uniformity of the external import tariffs of the participating countries, and suppression of an internal tariff line; pooling of customs revenues and their partition between the participating states in accordance with a formula established in advance. He claimed that the Austria-Modena arrangement failed to meet these conditions on every essential point: by leaving Modena free to add "internal" duties to the external ones, it in effect made provision for separate and distinct Austrian and Modena tariffs; it left a tariff wall between Austria and Modena; it failed to provide for community of customs revenues. He therefore demanded the extension to Sardinia of all the concessions granted by Austria to Modena.

De Buol, replying on behalf of Austria, claimed that the arrangement with Modena adequately met the conditions of a true customs union. Foreign goods crossing the territories of either Austria or Modena to reach the other member require only one and the same customs declaration, are subject to the same customs regulations, and pay only once the rates fixed by the tariff common to both countries. As for the internal duties, different in the two countries, *internal* arrangements between the parties have no bearing on the *international* character of the arrangement; the special internal duties have no international bearing, nor does the method of division of the revenues. International law does not establish any definition of a complete customs union; history furnishes too few precedents to make it proper to cite them on the meaning of this expression. The most important consideration in judging whether a tariff agreement is a customs union is the name given to it by the interested parties; to determine whether it is complete, all that is necessary is to see whether, after it is in operation, the two countries form, in their relations with the outside world, a single customs territory. If the conditions stated by Cavour must be met, then there has never been a complete customs union.[5] There are even single countries within which they are not met. While refusing, therefore, to concede the validity of the legal objections raised by Sardinia, De Buol stated that Austria, moved by other considerations, had asked Modena to accede to the nullification of the treaty.[6]

Prussia had also protested on behalf of the Zollverein, and, given the relations of the Zollverein and Austria at the time, this was probably a more powerful inducement to Austria to abandon the Modena treaty than the legal arguments of Cavour. The dispute with Sardinia nevertheless raised some difficult issues which were to arise again in the future. The express exemption of customs union from the obligations of most-favored-nation treatment in the Austria-Sardinia treaty had as a consequence that the question of the compatibility of customs union *per se* with most-favored-nation obligations could not be raised by Sardinia. It appears, however, that Austria's position was made weaker instead of stronger by the inclusion of this exception in the treaty with Sardinia in the form in which it there appeared. Had there been no mention at all of customs union, Austria might have contended on the basis of historical precedents that even an imperfect customs union was by general consent automatically exempt from most-favored-nation obligations. By specifically asking for exemption only for "complete" customs union,

---

5. He cited as conditions prevailing in the German Zollverein which were not in conformity with Cavour's requirements for a complete customs union: special duties on raw steel imported by way of the Baltic Sea, Swiss wines entering through Baden, butter imported into and for Saxony, and certain cloths entering by way of Prussia and Saxony; various transit duties; various duties on wines, spirits, etc., entering into one Zollverein state from another; salt trade restrictions; internal customs lines; special departures in the interest of particular states from the rules for general pooling of customs revenues.

6. For the text of the exchange of notes, see *Recucil des traités, conventions, et actes diplomatiques concernant l'Autriche et l'Italie* (Paris, 1859), pp. 731–36. Cf. also, P. Pradier-Fodéré, *Traité de droit international* (Paris, 1885–1906), IV, 418.

she put herself in what was probably an unnecessarily vulnerable position. The question as to how incomplete a customs union may be and still remain compatible with most-favored-nation obligations was to arise again.

By the Bulgaria-Serbia treaty of April 12, 1904, designated as a "treaty for customs union," the two signatory countries agreed to admit each other's domestic products free of duty and to follow similar customs policies toward third countries. Austria-Hungary, early in 1906, protested to Serbia against the treaty. Austria based its protest on its rights to most-favored-nation treatment in Serbia by virtue of the Congress of Berlin Act of 1878. It claimed that the treaty was incorrectly designated a "customs union" treaty, and demanded that this designation be eliminated from the treaty and all provisions removed from it which were in conflict with the most-favored-nation principle. Serbia yielded, and replaced the 1904 treaty by an ordinary commercial treaty.[7]

The questioning of the legality of the Austro-German Anschluss of 1931 turned predominantly on the compatibility of customs union with Austria's contractual obligation to maintain her political independence, and this phase of the customs union question will be dealt with in a subsequent section. Austria, however, had most-favored-nation obligations to a number of countries, and in the preliminary stages of the controversy there was some questioning of the compatibility of the Anschluss with these obligations. Both France and England argued before the Council of the League of Nations that there was strong ground to question the legality of customs union when there were outstanding

---

7. Cf. E. C. Helmreich, *The Diplomacy of the Balkan Wars, 1912–1913* (Cambridge, Mass., 1938), p. 9; Dušan Lončarević, *Jugoslaviens Entstehung* (Zurich, 1929), pp. 101 ff.; Dionys Jánossy, "Der handelspolitische Konflikt zwischen der österreichisch-ungarischen Monarchie und Serbien in den Jahren 1904–1910," *Jahrbuch des wiener ungarischen historischen Instituts* (Budapest), II (1932), 285–312 (not consulted).

most-favored-nation pledges which did not contain express exemption of customs union. In a memorandum submitted to the Council on May 18, 1931, the French Government made the following declaration on this point:

> If the régime arising out of the Protocol of March 19th should be of the nature of a Customs union, certain States will, in virtue of the most-favoured-nation clauses inserted in their treaties, certainly claim the Customs exemptions granted by Germany and Austria to one another. Although it may have been provided in several commercial treaties that the most-favoured-nation clause would not apply in the case of a Customs union, in others, on the contrary, this exemption is not mentioned; in this respect certain countries would have the strongest legal grounds for claiming in the present circumstances the full benefit of most-favoured-nation treatment.
>
> It is therefore probable that, if the Austro-German agreement were concluded, it would risk giving rise to grave disputes between States as to the application of the most-favoured-nation clause and provoking on one side or the other the denunciation of commercial treaties at present in force. The difficulties that might arise on this occasion would be so serious that it is for the Council to endeavor forthwith to prevent them.[8]

Czechoslovakia also charged violation of most-favored-nation obligations in the League Council discussions, and Austria made a routine denial.[9] Austria was in somewhat of a dilemma. To lessen the vulnerability of the Anschluss on the grounds of Austria's political obligations, it was expedient for her to minimize the

8. Cited from League of Nations, *Official Journal*, in Permanent Court of International Justice, *Customs Régime between Germany and Austria*, Series C, Pleadings, Oral Statements, and Documents, No. 53 (1931), pp. 620–21.

9. League of Nations, *Official Journal*, 1931, No. 7, Minutes, pp. 1075 ff.: 1069 ff.

closeness of the economic union which would result therefrom; to lessen the vulnerability of the Anschluss on the ground of its conflict with most-favored-nation obligations, it was expedient to claim its close conformity with the criteria of a perfect customs union. Before the Council of the League, therefore, Austria emphasized the completeness of the customs union, whereas before the International Court, where the question of most-favored-nation obligations was not pressed by the opposition, Austria stressed such retention of tariff autonomy under the Anschluss as the absence of a combined customs staff and the right—confined, as the majority opinion of the Court pointed out, to the formalities, since the Anschluss agreement provided for joint negotiations and for regard for the interests of the other party, and included an undertaking to the effect that one party will not ratify without the other—to conclude, sign, and ratify separately commercial treaties with outside countries.[10]

If the question of compatibility of customs union with most-favored-nation obligations were to be settled by appeal to precedents, few of the participants in the controversy would have been in a happy position if the full record had been brought into evidence. Austria herself had denied the compatibility of an incomplete customs union with most-favored-nation obligations in the Bulgaria-Serbia case of 1906, while the French Government had affirmed the compatibility of customs union with most-favored-nation obligations when its own customs

10. The majority opinion held that the régime proposed by the Anschluss certainly fulfilled the requirements of a customs union agreement as laid down by the Austrian Government itself in a memorial to the Court: "uniformity of customs law and customs tariff; unity of the customs frontiers and of the customs territory vis-à-vis third States; freedom from import and export duties in the exchange of goods between the partner States; apportionment of the duties collected according to a fixed quota." Manley O. Hudson, *ed., World Court Reports* (Washington, 1934–43), II, 723.

union with Monaco—a "complete" one, however—was at issue.[11] In the British position alone, apparently, was there complete historical consistency. The British Government has always maintained that, in the absence of an express exception, most-favored-nation obligations are a barrier to customs union. This apparently is still the British position today.[12]

3. The Most-Favored-Nation Principle Not a Serious Barrier to Customs Unions

If the customs unions are approximately "complete," however, it is not likely that most-favored-nation obligations would today be an obstacle. There is, first, the century-long record of customs unions which were permitted to operate without protest, or without successful protest. Second, many commercial treaties even in the nineteenth century contained an express exception of customs union from most-favored-nation obligations, and the practice of including such an exception became increasingly common in the twentieth century. Third, the League of Nations Secretariat repeatedly urged the general acceptance of compatibility between customs union and most-favored-nation obligations, and in 1933 the Economic Committee of the League included exemption of customs union in its suggested model

---

11. Cf. Gabriel Farnet, *Les relations douanières entre la France et la Principauté de Monaco* (Paris, 1917), p. 90.

12. Cf. Georg Schwarzenberger, "The Most-Favoured-Nation Standard in British State Practice," *British Year Book of International Law, 1945* (London, 1946), p. 109, note 5: "In the absence of an express reservation, a State can demand under the m.f.n. standard the benefits of exclusive preferential treaties, bilateral or multilateral, between the promisor and third States, such as customs unions which leave the international personalities of the contracting States intact."

most-favored-nation clause.[13] Finally, as will be shown later, the Havana Charter of the International Trade Organization, if brought into operation, will give customs unions, whether complete or partial, a substantially clear field. The question still remains, however, how complete need a customs union be in order to be exempt from most-favored-nation obligations?

Commercial treaties, moreover, can constitute a barrier to the formation of customs unions even if they do not contain a most-favored-nation pledge. The most formidable barrier would be a provision renouncing the right to enter a customs union without the consent of the other party, but the writer knows of only one such instance.[14] Provisions, such as are common in tariff treaties, stipulating maximum rates of duty or "binding" the rates of duty to be levied on imports from the other party would be a barrier, for the duration of the treaties, to entrance into a customs union any of whose rates of duty exceeded these maxima. However, this would not ordinarily be a serious barrier. Tariff treaties now invariably can be terminated within a short period if either party wishes. When the treaties run for substantial periods, as was common in the nineteenth century, a country bound by them can obtain special permission in the customs union agreement to maintain the lower rates until expiration of the obligation, as, for example, did Holstein-Luebeck in Article XII of the treaty of 1839, which brought her into the Zollverein, and Albania in the treaty of 1939 establishing customs union between Albania and Italy. If the period before unilateral termination becomes possible is too long to make this procedure acceptable to the other party or parties to a proposed

13. League of Nations, *Recommendations of the Economic Committee relating to Tariff Policy and the Most-Favoured-Nation Clouse* (Publication II. Economic and Financial, 1933, II. B.1), p. 21.

14. See *infra*, p. 84, note 4.

customs union, the country concerned may be able to secure release from its obligations, as happened in 1868 in the case of Mecklenburg-Schwerin, which obtained from France release from its obligations with respect to maximum rates of import duty on French products under a treaty which still had some ten years to run, in order to be free to enter the German Zollverein.

It may be objected that most-favored-nation obligations, should they be held to conflict with customs union, could be disposed of, in the same manner as provisions for maximum rates of duty, by termination of the treaties which establish them. In principle this is true, but in practice they have different status. In the first place, ordinary commercial treaties including the most-favored-nation clause but not including specific tariff-rate provisions are often signed to run for long periods before they can be unilaterally terminated. Secondly, maximum rates of duty are never obligatory, legally or otherwise, except by specific contract, whereas the principle of unconditional most-favored-nation treatment has for centuries carried great weight as a general principle which should govern international economic relations—even though fairly often departed from, and never until 1922 accepted at all by the United States. A country which would lightly terminate its obligation not to impose duties exceeding specified rates, even at the cost of surrendering corresponding claims against other countries, might nevertheless seriously hesitate before putting itself in a position where it could not claim most-favored-nation treatment from other countries on grounds either of contractual rights or of international comity.[15] It was the

15. If the most-favored-nation clause were in conditional form, the automatic exemption from it of customs union would presumably be easier to maintain than in the case of the unconditional form. But no case ever seems to have arisen where a country following the conditional practice has made claims against a member of a customs union on the strength of a commercial treaty containing the conditional most-favored-nation pledge, and with the abandonment by the United States of the conditional form and practice in 1922 it has ceased to have any practical significance.

most-favored-nation *principle* rather than most-favored-nation *pledges* that constituted the important barrier to preferential tariff arrangements in the past. The fact that customs union was generally regarded as compatible with most-favored-nation obligations had the result that customs union was promoted where otherwise some other form of preferential arrangement would have been chosen. If actual customs unions were nevertheless comparatively rare, it was because there were formidable barriers to mutual agreement to establish them, rather than because the most-favored-nation principle stood in the way.

Chapter III

Exemption from Most-Favored-Nation Obligations of Preferential Arrangements other than Customs Union

The widely prevalent desire of countries to escape from the full rigors of the most-favored-nation principle combined with the lack of willingness to do so by going the full length of customs union has led to sustained effort, largely successful, to establish the propriety of other types of relaxations of, or exceptions from, the most-favored-nation rule. These efforts are relevant here for two reasons: first, they have helped to obtain acceptance of less rigorous definitions of customs union than the traditional one and thus have exploited the general acceptance of derogation from the most-favored-nation principle for genuine customs union to win support for extending that derogation to types of tariff arrangement without valid claim to that designation; and second, by widening the range of types of tariff arrangement for which exemption from most-favored-nation obligations could he obtained, they have lessened the incentive to the formation of genuine customs unions.

The types of preferential tariff arrangements relevant here are: imperial preference; "regional agreements"; and "plurilateral agreements." Their most obvious distinguishing features are that: political ties are the special characteristic of imperial preference; propinquity, of regional agreements; and number of participants, of plurilateral agreements.

1. Imperial Preference

Preferential tariff relations short of customs union between the different territories of an empire go back at least to the early seventeenth century, have been present at some time in every empire of modern times possessing overseas colonies except the German pre-World-War-I empire and the Belgian one, and have been continuously present in some empires. It has until very recently always been generally taken for granted that preferential arrangements within an empire with common sovereignty fall outside the scope of the most-favored-nation clause: "unless there is a special stipulation to that effect, the most-favored-nation clause does not apply to special relations between colonies and mother countries."[1] Such special stipulations in the form of "open-door clauses" or their equivalent, have not been rare, and outside resentment against imperial preferences has been manifest since they first made their appearance; but except perhaps on the part of the United States in its first decades with respect to the British and French West Indies, and on the part of the United States and other countries later with respect to the relations of the autonomous British Dominions with Britain, it was universally recognized that they stood in a different category from preferential arrangements between politically independent countries.[2]

Imperial countries, therefore, have been free to set up customs unions within their territories without fear of

1. United States Tariff Commission, *Colonial Tariff Policies* (Washington, 1922), p. 26.

2. Perhaps in part because of misgivings about the compatibility of preferential relations between Great Britain and the British Dominions with the most-favored-nation principle after the Dominions had acquired full powers of self-government, exponents of British imperial preference were fond of applying the term "Zollverein" to the arrangements they were advocating although they fell far short of strict customs union in every essential respect. For a criticism of this practice, see Sir Robert Giffen, "The Dream of a British Zollverein," *Nineteenth-Century,* May, 1902, reprinted in Giffen, *Economic Inquiries and Studies* (London, 1904), II, 394–95.

most-favored-nation complications. In a few cases they have used this freedom; notably in the case of the "Ausgleich" between Austria and Hungary, but also in the case of the small customs unions between minor African colonies of Britain and of Belgium. Some writers would also include as customs union arrangements the practice of tariff assimilation between a mother country and a colony or colonies thereof, as in the cases of France and some of its colonies, of the United States and Puerto Rico, and of Japan and Formosa: "When the rates of duty of the tariff of the mother country are enforced also in the colony, the trade between these two units being free; that is, where mother country and colony form essentially a customs union, the tariff policy which prevails is that of assimilation."[3] From the economic point of view there is little or no difference between tariff assimilation and the ordinary customs union, the chief difference being that when tariff assimilation is introduced within an empire, it is invariably imposed by the mother country without having to be "negotiated," and the tariff is framed to suit the needs and wishes of the mother country's economy without much if any reference to the interests or wishes of the colonies. Another difference, whose economic significance depends upon the special circumstances prevailing, is that since colonies are practically always overseas, and often very far overseas, tariff assimilation unites for tariff purposes territories which are not contiguous.

For the most part, however, imperial preferences take other forms than tariff assimilation. They are in some cases the gradual product of several centuries of evolution, and even within an empire the forms and degrees of preference vary from colony to colony. Only one of these forms calls here for special mention. Since the Ottawa Agreement of 1932, the preferential relations

3. U. S. Tariff Commission, *Colonial Tariff Policies*, p. 33.

between Great Britain and the self-governing Dominions partake somewhat of the characteristics of a "plurilateral agreement."

The United States has since World War I been engaged in somewhat of a campaign against imperial preferences. In the Tariff Act of 1922 there was introduced a provision (Section 317) authorizing the President to impose additional duties or even outright prohibitions of import from countries discriminating against the trade of the United States in favor of other "foreign countries," but defining "foreign country" for the purposes of the section to mean "any empire, country, dominion, colony, or protectorate, or any subdivision or subdivisions thereof (other than the United States and its possessions), within which separate tariff rates or separate regulations of commerce are enforced." (It is, incidentally, characteristic of American attitudes towards customs union that tariff assimilation, which is very nearly the most extreme form of imperial preference possible, would not be covered by this definition.) This provision was retained in the Tariff Act of 1930 and is therefore still valid. It has never been invoked, and, to the writer's knowledge, there has never been any instance when its application has been seriously contemplated; its presence in the American tariff law has been only a gesture, but a gesture not wholly without significance. The United States believes in the "open door"—except in the case of Cuba and some of the American dependencies.

The reluctance of the United States to acknowledge the propriety of excepting imperial preferences from the equality-of-treatment principle has had its influence on the Havana Charter of the International Trade Organization. The signatory countries have, under American pressure, agreed that colonial preferences should be "eliminated," that is, that existing preferences should be reduced through a prescribed process of reciprocal bargaining, and that new ones should not be established nor old ones be increased. This is the only instance in modern times of the territorial scope of the most-favored-nation principle being enlarged; the whole trend of the times has been, as will be seen, to restrict it.

This now means, presumably, not that it is sufficient to put new preferential agreements in an outlawed category if they apply as between members of the same empire, but that to make them respectable they must also have some other characteristic which puts them in an approved category, as, for instance, if they are instances of tariff assimilation and therefore to be classed with customs unions, although it was no doubt contemplated at one time that the new trade charter should prohibit the formation of customs unions between territories of the same empire.[4]

2. Regional Agreements

Many countries inserted in their commercial treaties "regional clauses" exempting from most-favored-nation obligations any concessions granted to specified countries. The inclusion of such clauses frequently reflected little more than a sentimental contemplation of the desirability in the abstract of closer economic relations with countries with which there were—or it was pleasant to think that there were, or could be developed—specially close ties of sentiment and interest arising out of ethnological, or cultural, or historical political affiliations. Propinquity was usually a characteristic of the countries so related, as in the case of the "Balkan," "Nordic," "Central American," and other clauses, but not invariably. In the case of the "Nordic clause," Iceland was

4. The United States for a time in recent years was giving hearty encouragement to the formation of "plurilateral" agreements with exemption from most-favored-nation obligations, but more recently has ceased to do so. It would be easy to throw most systems of intra-imperial preference into the "plurilateral agreement" form. See *infra*, pp. 35 ff.

eligible for inclusion. In the case of the "Iberian clause," Brazil was included with respect to Portugal and the Spanish American republics with respect to Spain. In any case, the role of propinquity in the justification of such arrangements was largely a sentimental one, and often one based on false sentiment.

Neighborhood has never in international relations been a guarantee of, and often has been a deterrent to, neighborly feelings, and often this has not only been a fact but one too freely acknowledged. The adage that "good fences make good neighbors" was frequently in effect applied to peoples as well as to individuals. In the eighteenth century, and later, it was a stereotype in the literature on international relations.[5]

Economic factors, also, were on the whole not such as to make specially close commercial ties between neighboring countries genuinely attractive, since they were typically rival exporters of the same staple commodities and were not good sources of supply for the goods in most urgent demand from abroad. In the days of bad transportation facilities overland, or in regions of difficult terrain, a national tariff could cut off a town or village from its natural market to the serious and obvious injury of the inhabitants of both. But the "frontier clause," a common feature in commercial treaties, and other types of special provision for frontier trade, could be invoked to sanction an alleviation of the rigors, for the population living close to a national boundary, of a uniformly

5. The following citations are typical: Adam Smith, *Wealth of Nations*, [1776], Cannan ed., I, 460: "[France and England] being neighbours, they are necessarily enemies, and the wealth and power of each becomes, upon that account, more formidable to the other; and what would increase the advantage of national friendship, serves only to inflame the violence of national animosity." Henry Brougham, "Balance of Power," [1803], *Works* (Edinburgh, 1872), VIII, 39: "The circumstances which are found to constitute natural enmity between nations are threefold: *proximity* of situation, *similarity* of pursuits, and near *equality* of power." M. Drouyn de Lhuys to M. le prince de la Tour d'Auvergne, with respect to French designs on Tunis, France, *Livre jaune*, 1864, p. 143: "We are too much the friends of the Porte to wish to become its neighbours."

applied tariff—provided the smuggler did not render this service with adequate efficiency to make recourse to the frontier clause an unnecessary luxury.[6]

The consequence was that until recent years the privilege of entering into preferential arrangements which the regional clauses afforded was rarely exercised, and it is with some justification that they have been characterized as "Platonic clauses." During the inter-war years in Europe, however, and more recently in Latin America, they have been more widely made effective. In most cases the amount of trade affected by the preferences has been quite small, however, and, with a few possible exceptions, their increased use represents rather a phase of the general trend toward bilateralism during a difficult economic period than a movement of genuine importance toward economic unification on a regional basis.[7]

6. For special provisions for frontier trade, see T. E. Gregory, *Tariffs: A Study in Method* (London, 1921), pp. 411 ff.; U. S. Tariff Commission, *Dictionary of Tariff Information* (Washington, 1924), pp. 356 ff.; Richard C. Snyder, *The Most-Favored-Nation Clause* (New York, 1948), pp. 157–59.

7. The outstanding instances of use of a regional clause before World War I were, under the "Iberian clause," the commercial treaty between Portugal and Spain of March 27, 1893, which remained in effect until 1913, and provided for the reciprocal free entry of a specified list of commodities, and, under the "Cuban clause," the United States–Cuba reciprocity treaty of 1903, which with its successive renewals is still in effect, and which provides for exclusive reciprocal tariff concessions between the two countries.

For discussions of the merits of regional exemptions from most-favored-nation obligations, for the most part uncritically favorable, see Richard Riedl, *Exceptions to the Most-Favored Nation Treatment* (International Chamber of Commerce, Austrian National Committee: London, 1931), pp. 12 ff., and "Replies of National Committees and Memorandum on Dr. Richard Riedl's Report," International Chamber of Commerce, Washington Congress, 1931, *Document No. 12*.

For information relating to regional clauses in recent commercial treaties and their application, see *Customs Unions*, 1947, pp. 44–50. The special arrangements concluded in recent years, by virtue of these clauses, between Latin American countries seem for the most part to be ordinary "reciprocity" arrangements, but in the study cited (p. 49), the participating countries are said "to have evolved, or are evolving, in the direction of partial customs unions," and even the special relations

As long as the regional clauses were applicable only to pairs or groups of countries of which none, or at least not more than one, was in the first or even in the second rank in commercial importance, and perhaps also as long as there was solid ground for anticipating that the clauses would receive little or no application in practice, countries seeking to have such clauses included in their commercial treaties encountered little or no opposition, and such clauses, therefore, are numerous in the commercial treaties negotiated before World War I. During the great depression of the inter-war period, however, when movements for large regional blocs were being actively promoted in Europe, and especially when some of these were such as to have serious political as well as economic implications because of the size of the "region" involved and the proposed participation therein of a strong power with expansionist traditions, a note of hesitation and caution made itself heard in some quarters, and especially in Great Britain. The Ottawa Conference of 1932, which provided for a major extension of the system of British Empire preferential tariffs, with questionable taste adopted a formal resolution declaring that countries could not escape from their most-favored-nation obligations by forming regional pacts.[8] At the World Economic Conference held in London in 1933, Mr. Neville Chamberlain declared that the

---

between the United States and Cuba are given this new dignity. Whatever "to have evolved...in the direction of partial customs unions," may mean, these arrangements are for the most part substitutes for customs unions as means of escape from most-favored-nation obligations rather than steps towards them. See *infra,* pp. 36 and 71 ff., for further discussion of Latin American regionalism, and *infra,* pp. 121 ff., for some further comments on "regionalism" in general.

8. Great Britain, Parliamentary Papers, 1931–32, Cmd. 4174, pp. 25–26. In 1925, the British Government had defended its establishment, on behalf of its mandate, Palestine, of a preferential arrangement with Syria on the ground that such arrangements were customary between limitrophe countries, especially when they had once been under common sovereignty.

British Government would "find it difficult to agree to any formula allowing derogation from most-favoured-nation treatment
in respect of regional or group agreements" unless they were
"based on historical associations, such as were already generally
recognized," thus taking care of the only group agreements the
British Empire was interested in.[9]

3. Plurilateral Agreements

(a) The "Plurilateral Clause"

Closely related to the regional clause is the "plurilateral" or
"multilateral" clause, and they are not always clearly distin-
guishable. In the regional clause, proximity is generally implied
if not expressly required, the countries covered are further
limited in number, either by express specification of the countries eligible or by reference to some special affinity (economic,
geographic, political, or historical), and the number of countries eligible may be limited to two. In the plurilateral clause,
on the other hand, the emphasis, express or implied, is always
on the nonexclusiveness of the arrangement and on the substantial number of countries contemplated as members of a
prospective arrangement. There is sometimes expressed provision for open entry on equal terms, at least for countries which
can meet a broad geographical requirement. The purpose of
the clause remains identical with that of the regional clause,
namely, exemption from most-favored-nation obligations, but
the ground on which the claim to such exemption is made to
rest is now not the narrow territorial limitation of its scope

9. League of Nations, *Journal of the Monetary and Economic Conference*, 1933, p. 25.

but, on the contrary, its wide and potentially even unlimited territorial scope.

(b) Pre-World-War-I Proposals for European Tariff Union

Proposals for preferential tariff arrangements short of customs union but free from most-favored-nation obligations go back to the nineteenth century.[10] The earliest proposals of some consequence were made in the 1880s, aimed at some form of European economic union, and were openly directed, for the most part, against the United States. The American tariff was high and rising. By virtue of the most-favored-nation clause, the United States was claiming and receiving the benefit of the tariff reductions which European countries were granting to each other as the result of bilateral tariff bargaining. The United States itself, on the other hand, for the most part refrained from tariff bargaining, and when it did resort to it, it negotiated "reciprocity treaties" and refused, on the basis of its conditional interpretation of its own most-favored-nation pledges, even when they were formulated in unconditional—or in ambiguous—terms, to extend the resultant tariff reductions to third countries.[11] American exports of manufactured products were growing in volume, while the opening of the West and the reduction in transportation costs were bringing serious competition to European agriculture from American cereals and animal products. The competitive practices of the American "trusts" also gave rise to widespread criticism. The European press, in consequence, from

---

10. See, however, the Austrian ("Roxas") project of 1665, *infra*, p. 93.

11. See U. S. Tariff Commission, *Reciprocity and Commercial Treaties* (Washington, 1919), especially pp. 416–44, and Jacob Viner, "The Most-Favored-Nation Clause in American Commercial Treaties," *Journal of Political Economy*, XXXII (1924), 101–29.

the 1880's on resounded with complaints against the "American menace," or the "American invasion," and with proposals for concerted action to deal with it. The feeling was general in Europe that only concerted action could effectively cope with the problem, and that, moreover, single action by individual countries would face the hazard of strong American retaliation. There was, however, a natural reluctance on the part of European governments to take open leadership of a movement unlikely to succeed and involving the danger of punitive American action against the leaders of the movement if it failed.

The government of one European country, Austria, for whose products the American market was unimportant, so that American retaliation could not bring it much injury, did venture to supply leadership to the movement. In 1897, Count Goluchowski, the Austrian foreign minister, in a circular letter to other European countries, proposed that the countries of Europe combine to take concerted action directed against American commercial competition.[12] The anti-American orientation of his proposal was, if not overt, at least clearly enough implied in a publicly reported speech made by him that year before the Hungarian delegates to the Austro-Hungarian Parliament, which included the following passages:

> Europe has apparently reached a turning-point in her development. The solving of the great problem of the material well-being of nations, which becomes more pressing from year to year, is no longer a distant Utopia. It is near at hand. The disastrous competition which, in all domains of human activity, we have to submit to from over the seas, and which we will also have to encounter in the future, must be resisted if the vital interests of Europe are not to suffer, and if Europe

12. Cf. U. S. Tariff Commission, *Reciprocity and Commercial Treaties* (1919), p. 203.

is not to fall into gradual decay. Shoulder to shoulder we must ward off the danger that is at our doors, and in order to prepare for this we must draw upon all the reserves that stand at our disposal.

... the twentieth century will be a century of struggle for existence in the domain of economics. The nations of Europe must unite in order to defend their very means of existence. May that be understood by all, and may we make use of those days of peaceful development to which we look forward with confidence, to unite our best energies.[13]

(c) Allied Economic Conference, Paris, 1916

During World War I, but prior to American participation therein, France, England, and Italy, with France as the leader, agreed, at an Allied Economic Conference held at Paris, June, 1916, to take concerted action during and after the war in the field of commercial policy. This agreement was mainly directed against the Central Powers, but it was also a phase of a growing disillusion with the most-favored-nation principle and, in England, of the first stages of a reaction against its traditional free-trade policy. It was widely interpreted at the time in neutral countries, especially the United States, as an indication of the intention of the signatory countries to maintain for some time after the reestablishment of peace with the Central Powers preferential commercial relations with each other involving discrimination not only against the Central Powers but also, though to a lesser degree, against the neutral countries.

---

13. Cited in Alfred H. Fried, *The German Emperor and the Peace of the World* (New York, 1912), pp. 19–20.

The concern shown in neutral countries, and in free-trade circles within their own countries, upon the publication of the results of the deliberations of the Paris Conference, led to disclaimers, especially on the part of British statesmen, as to the correctness of the more extreme interpretations of the purport of the Conference's resolutions. These disclaimers, however, were in no instance clear and unambiguous, and they did not suffice to allay concern on the part of official Washington, including President Woodrow Wilson.[14]

There was ground for this concern, not only in the general atmosphere of hostility to the most-favored-nation principle by which the Paris Conference was surrounded, but because it was not plausible that the participants in the Conference, who well knew how closely its proceedings were being followed in neutral countries—though they failed to anticipate the extent of hostile reaction which its resolutions would arouse in neutral countries when they were published—would have had any difficulty in so formulating their resolutions as to make it clear that no discrimination against the trade of the neutrals was contemplated, had that in fact been true. But it was not true, as even the text of the resolutions of the Conference, guarded though its language was, suffices to show. The significant portion of the resolutions for present purposes was the second resolution under B, "Transitory Measures For the Period of . . . Reconstruction," and especially its second section, whose text read as follows:

Whereas the war has put an end to all treaties of commerce between the Allies and Enemy Powers, and whereas

---

14. A useful collection of material on the Paris Economic Conference of 1916 and its reception in various countries, is in National Foreign Trade Council, *European Economic Alliances* (New York, 1916).

it is of essential importance that, during the period of economic reconstruction which will follow the cessation of hostilities, the liberty of none of the Allies should be hampered by any claim put forward by the Enemy Powers to most-favored-nation treatment, the Allies agree that the benefit of this treatment shall not be granted to those Powers during a number of years to be fixed by mutual agreement among themselves.

During this number of years the Allies undertake to assure each other so far as possible compensatory outlets for trade in case consequences detrimental to their commerce result from the application of the undertaking referred to in the preceding paragraph.[15]

The entrance of the United States into the war on the side of the Allies, and the open hostility of the American Government to the letter and the spirit of the Paris resolutions, however, resulted in no action being taken by the Allies in the name of the Paris Conference, and as a binding text at least it was allowed to become inoperative. Traces of its influence, however, are easily to be found in the terms of the Peace Treaty with Germany, as well as in some of the trends of European commercial policy during the post-war period.[16]

---

15. The complete text is given in *ibid.*, pp. 24–29, and also in British *Parliamentary Papers,* Cd. 8271, 1916.

16. Etienne Clémentel, Minister of Commerce of the French Government, submitted in September, 1918, on behalf of France, a formal proposal for a revival of the Paris agreement, involving preferential arrangements, especially with respect to scarce raw materials, among the Allies for an indefinite period following the termination of the war, but was rebuffed by both the United States and Great Britain. See Etienne Clémentel, *La France et la politique économique interalliée* (Paris [1931]), pp. 337–48.

(d) The League of Nations and Plurilateral Agreements, 1927–1929

The idea of multilateral agreements on preferential trade relations remained alive in Europe during the post-war period, and received substantial though qualified support from the League of Nations and its agencies. The World Economic Conference, held at Geneva in 1927 under League of Nations auspices (it was not a "diplomatic" conference, however, and the delegates, even if officials, participated in their individual capacities), was the first of a series held during the inter-war period, all destined to have meager results. The Geneva Conference did not, in any of the resolutions finally adopted, deal explicitly with the question of multilateral tariff arrangements. It did recommend, however, in addition to unilateral and bilateral action, "collective action, by means of an enquiry, with a view to encouraging the expansion of international trade on an equitable basis by removing or lowering the barriers to international trade which are set up by excessive Customs tariffs,"[17] and also "the methodical examination, by the Economic Organisation of the League of Nations, of common measures which might be adopted, in the matter of tariffs, by States Members of the League and by States non-members, and also of the mutual agreements at which these States might arrive."[18] On the other hand, the Conference also "strongly" recommended "that the scope and form of the most-favoured-nation clause [in bilateral commercial treaties] should be of the widest and most liberal character and that it should not be weakened or narrowed either by express provisions or by interpretation."[19]

17. League of Nations, *Report and Proceedings of the World Economic Conference,* Geneva, 1927 (Document C.356.M.129.1927.II), I, 39.

18. *Ibid.,* I, 41.

19. *Ibid.,* I, 43.

Whether these recommendations could be reconciled (short of a multilateral convention of universal membership) and if so how, the Conference as a whole, in its general Report, made no attempt to answer.

In committee discussions, and in the presentation of views by delegates from particular countries, there was by no means uniform zeal for the maintenance—or rehabilitation—of the most-favored-nation principle, and proposals kept on cropping up for the exclusion of group agreements from the obligations of the most-favored-nation clause.

The most interesting suggestion in this connection was a proposal submitted by Mr. Riedl, a noted exponent of group agreements, on behalf of the Austrian Committee of the International Chamber of Commerce for "joint and parallel negotiations conducted between as large a group as possible of European States for the purpose of substantially lowering their Customs tariffs." The contracting states were to accord *each other* most-favored-nation treatment, but were apparently not to pledge most-favored-nation treatment to non-contracting states. "Without such assurance [of maximum tariff levels], a commercial treaty concluded on the basis of the most-favored-nation clause was merely a restriction which could become intolerable, and in some cases disastrous, since it permitted the other party to raise import duties still higher without any fear of retaliation. The most-favoured-nation clause, without the necessary guarantee with respect to tariffs, only led to a closed door."[20]

The League of Nations Assembly, its Secretariat, and various special League conferences which met over the next few years wrestled with this problem of how to reconcile or harmonize plurilateral preferential arrangements—especially if designed

20. *Ibid.*, II, 49.

to be confined to Europe, or to a specific part of Europe—with the most-favored-nation principle. The onslaught of the Great Depression intensified the search for a multilateral solution of the problem of the contagious intensification of barriers to trade, while the high tariff of the United States, raised still further by the Smoot-Hawley Act of 1930, and the American policy and practice of non-cooperation with the League's efforts to find a remedy for the prevailing economic warfare, added to other considerations to lead many European countries to look for the solution of their economic difficulties on a European rather than universal basis.[21]

The Assembly of the League had turned over to the Economic Committee of the League the task of carrying out the studies recommended by the Geneva Conference of 1927, and the Diplomatic Conference on the Abolition of Import and Export Prohibitions, at its 1928 meeting in Geneva, had asked the Economic Committee to inquire into the bearing of the most-favored-nation clause on the possibility of dealing effectively with the trade-barriers problem by means of multilateral agreements. The Economic Committee took this problem up at its 1929 meetings. In its report on the results of its deliberations, which it admitted were inconclusive, it commented, with admirable restraint, that "the World Economic Conference of Geneva, when it recommended the conclusion of plurilateral economic conventions with the object of improving the world economic situation and the application of the most-favoured-nation

---

21. For the relevant activities of the League and its agencies in these years, see Richard Riedl, *Exceptions to the Most-Favoured-Nation Treatment,* Report presented to the International Chamber of Commerce as documentation for its Washington Congress by the Austrian National Committee (London, 1931); League of Nations, *Commercial Policy in the Interwar Period* (Geneva, 1942), pp. 52–60; *Customs Unions,* 1947, p. 36; William E. Rappard, "Post-War Efforts for Freer Trade," *Geneva Studies,* IX (1938), No. 2.

clause in the widest and most unconditional form, probably did not quite realise that—up to a point—these two recommendations might clash."[22]

The Economic Committee reported that it had encountered the argument that it was necessary "to adopt a provision whereby the most-favored-nation clause embodied in bilateral commercial treaties would not, as a rule, affect plurilateral economic conventions," if countries were not to stay out of a plurilateral convention in the expectation that by insisting on their rights to most-favored-nation treatment they could enjoy its benefits without incurring its obligations. It, however, also reported the objection that some countries would be unwilling to give up their rights in this connection and might develop a hostile attitude towards the League's economic work if they were pressed to do so. It reached a compromise conclusion that a reservation from most-favored-nation obligations could be justified only in the case of plurilateral conventions "of a general character," only when expressly stipulated, and only when a state claiming the advantages of the plurilateral convention, though not acceding to it, "is not prepared to grant full reciprocity in the matter."[23]

A number of countries adopted the suggestion of the Economic Committee and introduced "plurilateral clauses" closely following the formulation suggested in their new commercial treaties.[24] In the Switzerland-Belgo-Luxemburg treaty of August 26, 1929, the clause read as follows:

ARTICLE 1. ...the most-favored-nation clause may not be invoked by the High Contracting Parties in order to obtain

22. League of Nations, *Recommendations of the Economic Committee Relating to Commercial Policy*, Geneva, 1929 (Document C.138.M.53.1929.II), p. 13.

23. *Ibid.*, pp. 13–14.

24. See Richard C. Snyder, *The Most-Favored-Nation Clause* (1948), pp. 166–68.

new rights or privileges which either of them may hereaf-
ter grant under collective conventions to which the other
is not a party, provided that the said conventions are concluded under the auspices of the League of Nations or [and?]
registered by it and open for the accession of the [?] States.
Nevertheless, the High Contracting Party concerned may
claim the benefit of the rights or privileges in question if
such rights or privileges are also stipulated in conventions
other than collective conventions which fulfil the aforemen-
tioned conditions, or if the Party claiming such benefits is
prepared to grant reciprocal treatment.[25]

The procedure of introducing plurilateral clauses into ordinary commercial treaties would take many years before it could

---

25. League of Nations, *Treaty Series,* CV(1930), 12–13. As *Customs Unions,* 1947,
p. 51, note 1, points out, other examples of this clause which are otherwise similar
leave out the "or" which the present writer has questioned above. Since registra-
tion of treaties with the League of Nations was a routine process, the substitution
of "and" for "or" would in effect impose a potentially significant limitation on the
exemption from most-favored-nation obligations. The word "the" which is here
questioned occurs in the League's English translation of the original French text,
where the wording is "des Etats." In the English translation given in *Customs Unions,*
1947, the wording is "all States."

A form of "plurilateral clause" appeared in earlier treaties, e.g., the United Kingdom
commercial treaties: with Spain, of October 31, 1922, and with Czechoslovakia,
of July 14, 1923. (See Martens, *Nouveau recueil général de traités,* 3d Series, XVII,
137, 284; and Richard C. Snyder, *loc. cit.*) In the United Kingdom–Spain commercial
treaty of October 31, 1922, the clause read as follows:

> "ARTICLE 23. This treaty shall not be deemed to confer any right or to impose
> any obligation in contravention of any general international convention to
> which His Britannic Majesty and His Catholic Majesty are or hereafter may
> be parties."

This article simply means, if here interpreted correctly, that a later general convention to which *both* are parties shall override the earlier treaty if there is conflict
between them. This type of plurilateral clause, therefore, did not meet the problem
of conflict between a bilateral treaty and a later plurilateral convention to which
only one of the signatories of the bilateral treaty was a party.

be completed, and one unrevised treaty could suffice to block the coming into effect of a plurilateral convention in conflict with it. There was considerable point therefore to the observation made in 1929 by the Austrian Government:

> ... it would not appear sufficient for the League merely to declare it legitimate to introduce a reservation in future treaties (or even by substitution in existing treaties); when a collective agreement has been concluded, it should request States not parties to such an agreement to refrain from claiming its benefits under the most-favored-nation clause unless they are prepared, while remaining outside the agreement, to assume its obligations.[26]

With the United States certain, however, and the United Kingdom likely, not only to stay out of, but to react against any plurilateral convention calling for lowering of trade barriers in accordance with some specified formula and stipulating that these reductions of duty are not to be extended to non-participants, the League was not prepared to take so daring a step.

(e) The Ouchy and Hague Conventions, 1932, 1937

The failure of the Ouchy Convention of 1932—although this was on the border line between a "regional" and a "plurilateral" agreement—was soon to provide a concrete illustration that the problem of conflict between plurilateral arrangements and most-favored-nation obligations had not been solved. Under this convention, negotiated at Ouchy but signed at Geneva, July 18,

---

26. *Austrian Government Observations on Recommendations of the Economic Committee Relating to Commercial Policy* (Doc. C.138.M.53.1929.II), L. N., Document (mimeographed) E.618, Geneva, September 26, 1930, p. 8.

1932, by Belgium, Luxemburg, and the Netherlands, the parties agreed that there should be no increases in existing duties or application of new duties on imports from each other; that no new duties on imports from other countries with which there were treaty relations should be levied unless those states had previously raised their own trade barriers; that existing duties on imports from each other should be reduced by 10 per cent per annum until the total reduction reached 50 per cent; that there should be no new barriers other than import duties on imports from each other; and that there should be open entry to the convention on the part of other countries and extension of its benefits to non-entering countries if they in fact carried out its terms.[27]

Of all the serious projects up to that time for collective tariff agreements, it went furthest in the direction of a genuine lowering of trade barriers. Belgium and the Netherlands, however, both had commercial treaties containing the most-favored-nation clause with the United Kingdom and other countries, and the Ouchy Convention provided that it should not come into effect until such countries had waived their rights. Great Britain refused to waive its rights; the Ottawa Conference held in the same year passed a resolution declaring that regional agreements could not be allowed to override most-favored-nation obligations; and the United States made no reply to the request for a waiver. The convention, in consequence, lapsed without ever coming into operation.

The Oslo group, which had organized in 1930 to pursue collective tariff reform, but had had no results of consequence, met again at The Hague, where they signed the Hague Convention

---

27. There is an excellent account of the Ouchy Convention in Erik Colban, *Mémoire sur la Convention Oslo* (documentation of the Bergen Conference of the International Institute for Intellectual Cooperation—mimeographed; Paris, 1939), pp. 39–47.

of May 28, 1937. The participating countries were the Ouchy Convention countries plus Norway, Sweden, Denmark, and Finland. The Hague convention provided for specified "bindings" of tariff rates, and for removals of specified existing quantitative restrictions on imports from participating countries and undertakings not to introduce new ones on commodities not already subject to them. All non-participating states were declared eligible to adhere to the convention in conformity with terms to be negotiated between them and the countries already parties thereto. It is to be noted that the convention did not provide for reductions, preferential or otherwise, of ordinary import duties, and it was presumably on the strength of this that the participating countries hoped that it would surmount the obstacle of the most-favored-nation clause.[28]

The Hague convention came into actual operation, but the Netherlands declined to renew it at the end of its first year of operation, and the other parties to it thereupon allowed it to lapse. The explanation offered by the Netherlands for its failure to renew its participation in the convention was that other countries, and especially the United Kingdom, had insisted that most-favored-nation obligations applied to quotas as well as to tariffs, that economic conditions had changed for the worse since the conclusion of the convention, which made its requirements irksome, and that the expected adherence of additional countries had not occurred.

The Netherlands and Belgium had meanwhile acceded to the request of the United Kingdom that favors granted to members of the convention should be extended also to it by virtue of its rights to most-favored-nation treatment. The

---

28. For the text, history, and analysis of the Hague Convention, see Erik Colban, *op. cit.*, pp. 54–72. The new importance of quantitative restrictions made this agreement potentially significant despite the absence from it of any provisions for tariff reductions.

Estonian and Latvian corresponding members of the Economic Committee of the League of Nations had also raised objections against the preferential removal of quotas on imports from the United Kingdom, apparently at a League Economic Committee meeting. They refused, moreover, to acknowledge that the convention met the standards of a plurilateral convention entitled to League recognition: it had not been concluded under the auspices of the League; it was not genuinely open to all states, since special prior negotiation was required to obtain accession.[29]

(f) Monetary and Economic Conference, London, 1933

Meanwhile, the problem had entered upon a new phase in 1933. The Roosevelt Administration had come into office in the United States and, under the leadership of Secretary of State Cordell Hull, proceeded to liberalize American commercial policy. The League of Nations, moreover, had summoned a World Monetary and Economic Conference to be held in 1933 in London, and the United States, while President Hoover was still in office, had agreed to participate. The question of plurilateral agreements was one of the problems on the agenda of the Conference.

The "Draft Annotated Agenda" prepared for the Conference by the Preparatory Commission of Experts, and dated January 20, 1933, gave a prominent place to this problem. After consideration of the procedures by which a general reduction of trade barriers could be negotiated and a declaration that "in normal conditions, the unconditional and unrestricted

---

29. See *Customs Unions,* 1947, p. 55, where the reply to these objections of an official spokesman for the Netherlands is also reported.

most-favoured-nation clause should form the basis of commercial relations between nations," it took up the question of what exceptions, permanent and temporary, to the clause were desirable, and in this connection gave special attention to the question of whether the terms of plurilateral agreements should be permanently exempted from the clause. The relevant section of the Draft Agenda read as follows:

V.—B. Most-Favoured-Nation Clause
(a) Permanent Exceptions

Certain permanent exceptions to the clause are already usual in treaties of commerce (frontier traffic, Customs unions, etc.). Careful attention should, however, be paid to the question whether other permanent exceptions should be admitted, particularly as regards rights derived from collective agreements.

A suggestion which has been strongly pressed in various quarters is that States should admit an exception to the most-favoured-nation clause whereby advantages derived from plurilateral agreements should be limited to the contracting States and to such States as may voluntarily grant equivalent advantages. This proposal (which has already been adopted in certain bilateral treaties) should certainly be most carefully studied. It has been argued, in support of this proposal, that, in the absence of an exception of this kind, the conclusion of collective conventions would encounter insuperable difficulties, since the application of the clause would, in such circumstances, place a premium on abstention. On the other hand, it has to be borne in mind that the circumstances of various countries differ considerably, so that in many cases they could not adhere to a plurilateral agreement when they are unaware of the concrete cases to which its provisions might later be applied and of the possible consequences which its application might involve for themselves. Moreover, there would be a danger of provoking the formation of mutually opposed groups of countries, thus aggravating the very evils which it is sought to mitigate. Finally, it has been emphasized that care must be taken to avoid prejudicing the rights of third parties.

In any case, these exceptions must be subject to the conditions that agreements of this kind be open to the adhesion of all interested States and that their aim should be in harmony with the general interest. Amongst the conditions that might be considered for this purpose, mention may be made of a proviso that these agreements shall have been concluded under the auspices of the League of Nations or of organisations dependent on the League. Further, these agreements must not involve new hindrances to international trade *vis-à-vis* countries having most-favoured-nation rights. Finally, "collective agreements" can only be regarded as such when they comply with certain conditions, to be determined, as to the number of the participating States.

The Conference should endeavour to find a solution for the whole of this question which will reconcile the interests of all.[30]

These suggestions represent in substance a crystallization of the conclusions which the League and its Secretariat had been

---

30. League of Nations, Monetary and Economic Conference, *Draft Annotated Agenda Submitted by the Preparatory Commission of Experts,* Geneva, 1933 (League Document C.48.M.18.1933.II. [Conference Document M.E.I.]), pp. 30–31.

developing since 1927, and this portion of the Draft Agenda no doubt owed much to the League officials who helped in its preparation. The American representation on the Preparatory Commission of Experts included no tariff expert. On the assumption that the Monetary and Economic Conference would succeed in framing an economic charter to which most of the countries of commercial importance in the world would subscribe, the difficulties encountered by the Ouchy and Hague conventions in avoiding conflict with most-favored-nation obligations to non-members would not be encountered by a collective agreement negotiated subsequent to the conclusion and ratification of a Conference convention embodying the suggestions of the Preparatory Commission of Experts. The sole element in the Preparatory Commission's suggestions which appears not to have been brought forward in previous discussions was the point made that to meet the requirements of a "collective agreement" there must be a minimum number of participating states. Significant also was the absence of any reference to "regional" agreements. The emphasis in the Commission's suggestions was thus on *number* of participants instead of on proximity or geographical location of participants, as had often been the case in previous discussions of the problem.

A major difficulty in the past in reaching agreement as to preferred status for collective arrangements arose, on the one hand, out of the desire to obtain arrangements in which the United States would not be a participant and, indeed, which would have as an important objective concerted action to cope with American competition in foreign trade, and, on the other hand, out of the fear that the United States, whether it was welcome as a participant or not, would not only refuse to participate in, but would vigorously oppose any such arrangement. Full cooperation of the United States in the deliberations of the

Conference, at least until its final débacle, promised to remove at least the second aspect of this difficulty. Further ground for optimism on both scores was provided when Secretary Hull submitted a provision for adoption by the Conference which not only contained in substance all the suggestions of the Preparatory Commission but indicated that American approval would be forthcoming for collective agreements which in practice would be limited in their geographical scope. The provision proposed by Secretary Hull for adoption by the Conference read as follows:

> The participating Governments urge the general acceptance of the principle that the rule of equality shall not require the generalisation to non-participants of the reduction of tariff rates or import restrictions made in conformity with plurilateral agreements that give reasonable promise of bringing about such general economic strengthening of the trade area involved as to prove of benefit to the nations generally; provided such agreements:
>
> (a) Include a trade area of substantial size;[31]
> (b) Call for reductions that are made by uniform percentages of all tariff rates or by some other formula of equally broad applicability;
> (c) Are open to the accession of all countries;
> (d) Give the benefit of the reductions to all countries which in fact make the concessions stipulated; and
> (e) When the countries party to the plurilateral agreement do not, during the term of the plurilateral treaty, materially

---

31. This was from an economic point of view an improvement on the Preparatory Commission's stress on *number* of participants, since number is of economic significance only as it involves size. See *infra*, p. 51.

increase trade barriers against imports from countries
outside of such agreements.[32]

This proposal covered all the significant points made in the
Draft Agenda and added other points which had been raised
in previous discussions of the problem. As a proposal to facilitate the negotiation of collective agreements, however, it had
what in the light of previous and subsequent experience must
be regarded as two major defects. First, instead of proposing
that the "participating governments urge the general acceptance" of the principle formulated, it should have proposed
that the participating governments adopt it there and then.
The innocuousness of vague appeals by general conferences for
good behavior should by this time have been apparent to all.
Secondly, the requirement that the reductions of tariffs called
for by collective agreements should be according to a formula
failed to anticipate future experience. It was no doubt intended
to give real force to the requirement of open entry. But the differences in trade-barrier levels, and in economic conditions,
and the strength in all countries of specific vested interests in
protection, make acceptance of reduction of trade barriers by a
percentage formula across the board or by any correspondingly
inflexible formula more than can be realistically expected of
most countries. The only instance of success in reaching agreement on such a pattern of trade-barrier reduction was in the
case of the Ouchy Convention, and in this case only three countries were involved. The Hague Convention, based on bilateral
bargaining, and, more emphatically, the successful bilateral

32. League of Nations, Monetary and Economic Conference, *Reports Approved by the
Conference on July 27th, 1933, and Resolutions Adopted by the Bureau and the Executive
Committee*, London, 1933 (League Document C.435.M.220.1933.II. [Conference
Document M.E.22(1)]), p. 43.

bargaining in a multilateral framework at Geneva in 1947, in which eighteen countries participated, would not have met the requirements for eligible collective agreements laid down in Secretary Hull's proposals, but the procedure followed at The Hague and at Geneva appears to be the only practicable one whereby the reduction of trade barriers in a multilateral setting can be procured with reasonable speed.

The London Conference, however, was not only fated to be an addition to the already long list of abortive international economic conferences but, as the result of President Roosevelt's famous message blasting the currency stabilization proposals before the Conference, it was destined to collapse without even the standard amount of pretense that it had succeeded in accomplishing anything of consequence.

(g) Inter-American Resolutions and Agreements, 1933–1948

Later in the same year, at the Montevideo Conference of the American States, Secretary Hull submitted and obtained the adoption in principle of a draft agreement having much in common with the proposal which he had submitted to the London Conference but which was free from the two defects referred to above: The Montevideo resolutions (Nos. V and LXXXI) were in themselves—if signed and ratified—a definite undertaking not to invoke the most-favored-nation clause in connection with multilateral agreements, and not merely a recommendation to the signatory governments; the resolutions did not call for reduction of trade barriers in accordance with a formula. After some slight modifications in the draft agreement had been made by the Governing Board of the Pan American Union, it was opened to signature by all countries. Up to the end of 1939, it had been signed by eight countries, including two European countries, and ratified by two countries, the United States and Cuba.[33]

At the Third Meeting of Ministers of Foreign Affairs of the American Republics, held at Rio de Janeiro in January, 1942, among the resolutions adopted were one (No. VII) which recommended to the Governments of the American Republics that they "study the desirability of making an exception in the commercial agreements which they conclude with nations outside the Western Hemisphere of the treatment which they extend in commercial and customs matters to all of the other American Republics," and another (No. XIV) which recommended that the American Republics "study promptly the possibility of concluding a multilateral convention binding themselves not to claim, by virtue of the most-favored-nation clause, concessions and facilities which each of them may grant or may have granted to the commerce of the inland countries of the Americas [i.e., Bolivia and Paraguay] in order to eliminate or minimize the disadvantages inherent in the geographical position of such countries." These resolutions were not accepted by the United States, presumably as inconsistent with the most-favored-nation principle and with appropriate regional or multilateral exceptions therefrom. The American delegates made a formal reservation, in the following terms:

---

33. See "Agreement between the United States of America and Other Powers concerning the Nonapplication of Most-Favored-Nation Clause in respect of Certain Multilateral Economic Conventions," opened for signature July 15, 1934, U. S. *Statutes at Large,* Vol. 49, Pt. 2, pp. 3260–66; U. S. *Treaty Series* 898. For texts of the resolutions referred to, see *The International Conferences of American States: First Supplement, 1933–1940* (Washington: Carnegie Endowment for International Peace, 1940), pp. 20–22, 96–97; also U. S. Department of State, *Treaty Information Bulletin,* No. 51 (December, 1933), p. 8; No. 52 (January, 1934), pp. 20–21.

The Government of the United States of America desires to have recorded in the Final Act its reservation to Resolution VII...and Resolution XIV..., since the terms of these Resolutions are inconsistent with the traditional policy of liberal principles of international trade maintained by the United States of America and as enunciated and reaffirmed at the recent International Conferences of American States and the First and Second Meetings of the Ministers of Foreign Affairs of the American Republics.[34]

The Economic Agreement of Bogotá, signed on May 2, 1948, at the Ninth International Conference of American States, included, as Article 31, the following provision:

States with common boundaries or those belonging within the same economic region, may conclude preferential agreements for purposes of economic development, each State respecting the obligations that it has undertaken by virtue of existing international bilateral agreements or multilateral agreements that have been or may be concluded. The benefits granted in such agreements shall not be extended to other countries by application of the most-favored-nation clause, except in case of a special agreement in that respect.

---

34. "Third Meeting of Ministers of Foreign Affairs of the American Republics," Rio de Janeiro, January, 1942, Carnegie Endowment for International Peace, *International Conciliation,* No. 378 (March, 1942), pp. 116–117, 120, 143. The First Meeting of the Ministers of Foreign Affairs was held in 1939 and the Second in 1940. The relevant resolutions adopted at these meetings called simply for adherence to the most-favored-nation principle, with no reference to inter-American preferential arrangements.

This provision would remove from the operation of the most-favored-nation clause not only "regional" and "pluri-lateral" preferences but also bilateral reciprocity agreements between non-contiguous countries, provided only they were within the "same economic region," a term which might, in the context of the Bogotá Economic Agreement as a whole, apply to the entire Western Hemisphere. An interesting reservation to Article 31 made by the Delegation of Ecuador maintained that the article should be interpreted as permitting preferences between Spanish-American States whether for economic or for non-economic reasons. The text of the Ecuadorian reservation is as follows:

> Article 31 must be understood in the sense that preferences between Spanish-American States are permitted, either for economic reasons—due to the need for the development of their economies and because they belong to the same region—or because such preferences concern States united among themselves by special ties based on a community of language, origin, and culture.

The Delegation of the United States entered a formal reservation to Article 31.[35]

The "Quito Charter," or Agreement with a View to the Establishment of a Greater Colombia Economic and Customs Union, signed at Quito August 9, 1948, by Colombia, Ecuador,

---

35. For the text of the Economic Agreement of Bogotá, see *Ninth International Conference of American States, Bogotá, Colombia, March 30–May 2, 1948; Report of the Delegation of the United States of America, with Related Documents*, U. S. Department of State, Publication 3263.

Panama, and Venezuela, referred in its preamble to Article 31 of the Economic Agreement of Bogotá in the following terms:

> Considering that in accordance with the Economic Agreement of Bogotá, neighboring American States or States belonging to the same economic region may conclude preferential agreements for purposes of economic development;

Article 28 of the Quito Charter no doubt has reference to the possibility of conflict with the Havana Charter. It reads as follows:

> The Contracting Governments undertake jointly to secure, if necessary, the acceptance by other states of the system established by the provisions of the present Agreement and to defend this Agreement before the competent international organizations.

Article 29 permits, subject to unanimous decision, accession to the Agreement by any Spanish-American state, "having regard to the special links which unite the Hispano-American States in view of their community of origin and culture," but with the proviso "that the State expressing its desire to accede is at a stage of economic development similar to that of the Associated States." Other American states "which are or which may be in a similar position" may also be allowed to accede. In other words, of the Western Hemisphere sovereign countries, none are *ipso facto* ineligible for membership except the United States and Canada.

The Quito Charter provides for an elaborate consultative and drafting organization with a view, among other things, to the establishment of customs union between the member countries, but it is clear that it contemplates, at least for an interim period, the establishment of trade relations between the members on a preferential basis falling far short of customs union.[36]

The bearing of the Havana Charter for an International Trade Organization on the most-favored-nation clause in relation to plurilateral agreements is examined in a subsequent section of this study.

---

36. The text of the Quito Charter used is the translation supplied by the Division of Conferences and Organizations of the Pan American Union.

Chapter IV

The Economics of Customs Unions

1. Customs Union as an Approach to Free Trade

The literature on customs unions in general, whether written by economists or non-economists, by free-traders or protectionists, is almost universally favorable to them, and only here and there is a sceptical note to be encountered, usually by an economist with free-trade tendencies. It is a strange phenomenon which unites free-traders and protectionists in the field of commercial policy, and its strangeness suggests that there is something peculiar in the apparent economics of customs unions. The customs union problem is entangled in the whole free-trade–protection issue, and it has never yet been properly disentangled.

The free-trader and the protectionist, in their reasoning about foreign trade, start from different premises—which they rarely state fully—and reach different conclusions. If in the case of customs unions they agree in their conclusions, it must be because they see in customs unions different sets of facts, and not because an identical customs union can meet the requirements of both the free-trader and the protectionist. It will be argued here that customs unions differ from each other in certain vital but not obvious respects, and that the free-trade supporter of customs union expects from it consequences which if they were associated in the mind of the protectionist with customs union would lead him to oppose it. It will also be argued, although with less conviction because it involves judgments about quantities in the absence of actual or even possible measurement, that with respect to most customs union projects the protectionist is right and the free-trader is wrong in regarding the project as something, given his premises, which he can logically support.

To simplify the analysis, it will at first be confined to perfect customs unions between pairs of countries; and the "administrative" advantages of customs unions, such as the shortening of customs walls, and the "administrative" disadvantages, such as the necessity of co-ordinating customs codes and of allocating revenues by agreed formula, will be tentatively disregarded. Also, to separate the problem of customs unions *per se* from the question of whether in practice customs unions would result in a higher or in a lower "average level" of duties[1] on imports into the customs union area from outside the area, it will be assumed that the average level of duties on imports from outside the customs area is precisely the same for the two countries, computed as it would be if they had not formed the customs union. It will at first be assumed that the duties are of only two types:[2] (*a*) "nominal duties," that is, duties which have no effect on imports because there would be no imports of commodities of the kind involved even in the absence of any import duties on them;[3] and (*b*) "effective protective duties," that is, duties which operate to reduce imports not only by making commodities of the specific kind involved more expensive to

1. Whether it is possible to give this concept of an "average level" of duties both some degree of precision of definition and economic significance is taken up later. See *infra,* pp. 66–68.

2. "Revenue duties" are dealt with subsequently. See *infra,* pp. 65–66.

3. Such duties, while they have no effect on imports, can have other effects of some economic importance, though these are not directly relevant here. In countries where an approach to perfect competition does not prevail, which means most countries, import duties may protect monopolistic or government-supported domestic price levels instead of protecting domestic production.

potential consumers and so lessening their consumption, but also, and chiefly, by diverting consumption from imported commodities to the products of corresponding domestic industries. The analysis will be directed toward finding answers to the following questions: in so far as the establishment of the customs union results in change in the national locus of production of goods purchased, is the net change one of diversion of purchases to lower or higher money-cost sources of supply, abstracting from duty-elements in money costs: (*a*) for each of the customs union countries taken separately; (*b*) for the two combined; (*c*) for the outside world; (*d*) for the world as a whole? If the customs union is a movement in the direction of free trade, it must be predominantly a movement in the direction of goods being supplied from lower money-cost sources than before. If the customs union has the effect of diverting purchases to higher money-cost sources, it is then a device for making tariff protection more effective. None of these questions can be answered *a priori,* and the correct answers will depend on just how the customs union operates in practice. All that *a priori* analysis can do, is to demonstrate, within limits, how the customs union must operate if it is to have specific types of consequence.

The removal of "nominal" duties, or duties which are ineffective as barriers to trade, can be disregarded, and attention can be confined to the consequences of the removal, as the result of customs union, of duties which previously had operated effectively as a barrier, partial or complete, to import.

There will be commodities, however, which one of the members of the customs union will now newly import from the other but which it formerly did not import at all because the price of the protected domestic product was lower than the price at any foreign source plus the duty. This shift in the locus of production as between the two countries is a shift from a high-cost to a lower-cost point, a shift which the free-trader can properly approve, as at least a step in the right direction, even if universal free trade would divert production to a source with still lower costs.

There will be other commodities which one of the members of the customs union will now newly import from the other whereas before the customs union it imported them from a third country, because that was the cheapest possible source of supply even after payment of duty. The shift in the locus of production is now not as between the two member countries but as between a low-cost third country and the other, high-cost, member country. This is a shift of the type which the protectionist approves, but it is not one which the free-trader who understands the logic of his own doctrine can properly approve.[4]

Simplified as this exposition is, it appears to cover most of the basic economic issues involved. The primary purpose of a customs union, and its major consequence for good or bad, is to shift sources of supply, and the shift can be either to lower- or to higher-cost sources, depending on circumstances. It will be noted that for the free-trader the benefit from a customs union to the customs union area as a whole derives from that portion of the new trade between the member countries which is wholly

4. A third possibility should be mentioned. The import duty on a particular commodity may be so high in one of the countries that it is prohibitive of import, but domestic production may be impossible or excessively costly, so that there is no consumption. Upon formation of the customs union, the commodity in question may be imported from the other member country, where its cost of production may be high or low as compared to costs elsewhere but is assumed to be lower than outside costs plus the duty on imports from outside the customs union. The original duty thus served as a sumptuary measure rather than as a protective or revenue measure. Whether the removal of a sumptuary measure is of benefit for the country particularly concerned as potential consumer is not a type of question which the economist has any special capacity to answer. But if as the result of customs union country A removes a duty of this kind preferentially for imports from the other member country, B, there is a clear loss for A as compared to the removal of duty regardless of source if B is a high-cost source of supply. There is an unquestionable benefit here, however, for the supplying country, and it does not injure outside countries in any direct way.

new trade, whereas each particular portion of the new trade between the member countries which is a substitute for trade with third countries he must regard as a consequence of the customs union which is injurious for the importing country, for the external world, and for the world as a whole, and is beneficial only to the supplying member country. The protectionist, on the other hand, is certain to regard the substitution of trade between the member countries for trade with third countries as the major beneficial feature of customs union from the point of view of the participating countries and to be unenthusiastic about or even to regard as a drawback—at least for the importing country—the wholly new trade which results from the customs union.

From the free-trade point of view, whether a particular customs union is a move in the right or in the wrong direction depends, therefore, so far as the argument has as yet been carried, on which of the two types of consequences ensue from that custom union.

Where the trade-creating force is predominant, one of the members at least must benefit, both may benefit, the two combined must have a net benefit, and the world at large benefits; but the outside world loses, in the short-run at least, and can gain in the long-run only as the result of the general diffusion of the increased prosperity of the customs union area. Where the trade-diverting effect is predominant, one at least of the member countries is bound to be injured, both may be injured, the two combined will suffer a net injury, and there will be injury to the outside world and to the world at large. The question as to what presumptions can reasonably be held to prevail with respect to the relative importance in practice of the two types of effects will be examined subsequently.

To the reasoning presented above, there is one qualification in favor of customs union which needs to be made, on which both free-traders and protectionists can with reason find some common ground, although, in the opinion of the writer, they both tend to exaggerate its importance for the customs union problem. It has here been assumed hitherto that in so far as a customs union has effects on trade these must be either trade-creating or trade-diverting effects. This would be true if as output of any industry in a particular country increases over the long-run relative to the national economy as a whole, its money costs of production per unit relative to the general level of money costs also tended to rise. Economists are generally agreed, however, that there are firms, and consequently also industries, where this rule does not hold but instead unit costs decrease as output expands. From this they conclude that where a small country by itself, because of the limited size of its domestic market (and, it should be added, the prevention by foreign tariffs of its finding a market outside), may be unable to reach a scale of production large enough to make low unit-costs of production possible, two or more such countries combined may provide a market large enough to make low unit-cost production possible. If an industry which thus expands, whether from zero or from a previous small output, is in country A, and the other member of the customs union is country B, the diversion of B's imports from a country, C, outside the customs union to country A, may be a beneficial one for B as well as for A, and, moreover, there may be suppression of trade, namely, of the imports of A from C of the commodity in question, which may also be beneficial to A. Whether such diversion—and suppression—of trade will, from the free-trade point of view, be beneficial or injurious to A will depend on several circumstances. The cost of production in A of the commodity in question is now lower than it was before. There is gain, therefore, for A as compared to the precustoms-union situation with respect to that portion of its present output which corresponds to its previous output (which may have been zero), and there is clear gain on such of its additional output as is now exported to B. On additional output beyond this, however, there is loss to A if the new cost, though lower than the previous one, is higher than the cost (before duty) at which it is obtainable from C, but there is additional gain to A if the new cost is lower than the cost (before duty) at which it is obtainable from C. For B, there is loss by the amount imported by B times the per unit amount by which A's price exceeds the price at which B's import needs could be supplied by C; there is gain to B only if A's price is now lower than C's price (before duty). There is thus a possibility—though not, as is generally taken for granted in the literature, a certainty—that if the unit-cost of production falls as the result of the enlarged protected market consequent upon customs union there will be a gain from customs union for one of the members, for both the members, and/or for the union as a whole, but there is also a possibility—and often a probability—that there will be loss in each case.

It does not seem probable that the prospects of reduction in unit-costs of production as the result of enlargement of the tariff area are ordinarily substantial, even when the individual member countries are quite small in economic size. The arguments for substantial economies from increased scale of industry presented by economists rest wholly or mostly on alleged economies of scale for *plants* or *firms,* and on the assumption that large-scale plants or firms are not practicable in small *industries* and therefore in small countries. It seems to the writer unlikely, however, that substantial efficiency-economies of scale of plant are common once the plants are of moderate size, and he is convinced that in most industries plants can attain or approach closely their optimum size for efficiency even though the industries are not large in size. Were it not for trade barriers, moreover, even small countries could have large industries.

There are few industries, even in countries where large-scale production is common, in which there are not plants of moderate size which are as efficient, or nearly as efficient, measured in unit-costs, as the giant plants; and there are few giant firms which do not maintain some of their plants, presumably at a profit, on a moderate scale. There are few manufacturing industries—and the economies of scale of plant or industry are generally conceded to be confined mainly or only to such industries—which have not been able to maintain themselves on a low-cost basis in one or more small countries, such as Switzerland, Sweden, Denmark, or Belgium. If the applicability of this argument is confined to products which nowhere are produced at a low unit-cost from plants which are quite small, either absolutely or as compared to the maximum size elsewhere, the scope of the argument is much more limited than is commonly taken for granted. It may be asked in rebuttal, how then explain the existence of giant plants and giant firms? It is at least a partial answer: (1) as to size of plants, that the survival of plants of moderate size in competition with the giant plants calls equally for explanation; and (2) as to size of firms, that there are in an imperfectly competitive world many incentives to growth in size of firm even at the cost of efficiency in production—firms of quite undistinguished records in efficiency of production have been known to grow by absorption of more efficient smaller firms and by the use of monopoly power in buying and in retention of customers, and, generally speaking, growth in size is more often the result of efficiency than contributory to efficiency.

The general rule appears to be that once an industry is large enough to make possible optimum scale—and degree of specialization of production—in plants, further expansion of the industry in a national economy of constant over-all size is bound to be under conditions of increasing unit-costs as output increases, in the absence of new inventions. To expand, the industry must draw away from other industries increased amounts of the resources it uses, and consequently must pay higher prices per unit for resources of the type which it uses more heavily than does industry at large, and must reduce the extent to which it uses them relative to other types of resources, thus bringing into operation the law of diminishing returns. It may be objected that this will not hold true in the case of a customs union, since this in effect increases the over-all size of the "national" economy. It is the supply conditions of factors of production, however, which are the relevant restrictive factor on expansion of output of an industry without increase of unit-costs, and unless customs union appreciably increases the inter-member mobility of factors of production it does not in this sense increase the "scale" of the "national" economy from the point of view of production conditions even if it does increase it from the point of view of the size of the protected market for sales.

Few free-traders have dealt with the economics of customs unions in any detail, and one must resort in some measure to inference from the implications of brief dicta to find the explanation for their general support of customs union as constituting an approach to their ideal of the territorial allocation of production in accordance with comparative costs of production. The major explanation seems to lie in an unreflecting association on their part of any removal or reduction of trade barriers with movement in the direction of free trade. Businessmen, however, and governments which have had to try simultaneously to satisfy both special interests seeking increased protection and voters hostile to protection, have long known of ways of making increased protection look like movement in a free-trade direction. They have known how, under suitable circumstances, protection against foreign competition could be increased by *reducing* duties and reduced by increasing duties. Let us suppose that there are import duties both on wool and on woolen cloth, but that no wool is produced at home despite the duty. Removing the duty on wool while leaving the duty unchanged on the woolen cloth results in increased protection for the cloth industry while having no significance for wool-raising. Or suppose that the wool is all produced at home, and sold to domestic clothmakers at the world price plus duty, but would be all produced at home even if there were no duty on wool, but would then be sold at the world price. Removal of the duty on wool again increases the protection for the woolen industry without reducing the volume of domestic production of wool.

When the customs union operates to divert trade from its previous channels rather than to create new trade, the partial removal of duties which it involves operates in analogous manner to increase the protective effect for high-cost producers of the duties which remain, not, however, by reducing imports into their own national territory but by extending the operation in their favor of the protective duty to the territory of the other partner of the customs union. It would in theory be possible that if two areas were joined in customs union, the customs union would have no trade-creating effect and only trade-diverting effect, i.e., no industry in either area would meet with new competition from the other area, while some high-cost industries, existing or potential, in each area would acquire a new set of consumers in the other area who would be placed at their mercy because the customs union tariff will now shut them off from low-cost sources of supply. A set of connected tariff walls can give more market-dominance to high-cost producers than a set of independent tariff walls, if the former set has had its internal sections knocked out.

This is well, though ingenuously, brought out in one of the leading treatises in favor of customs unions, where the author, after arguing that free-traders should like them because they eliminate trade barriers, proceeds to argue that protectionists should also like them because of the extension of the (protected) market area which they provide for producers within the territory of the customs union; "as for the internal competition, it will not be formidable if care is exercised in choosing as partners in customs unions countries which are complementary [in production] rather than competitive."[5]

Free-traders sometimes in almost the same breath disapprove of preferential reductions of tariffs but approve of customs unions, which involve 100 per cent preference, and this is the position at present of the United States Government and the doctrine of the Havana Charter.[6] If the distinction is made to rest, as often seems to be the case, on some supposed virtue in a 100 per cent preference, which suddenly turns to maximum evil at 99 per cent, the degree of evil tapering off as the degree of preference shrinks, it is a distinction as illogical, the writer believes,

---

5. L. Bosc, *op. cit.*, p. 98. He moves on to a perfect *non sequitur:* "Thanks to this judicious choice, *there will be established within the customs union a fecund division of labor,* while the customs frontiers thus extended further territorially will protect the internal market against the superiority of other countries." (Italics supplied.)

6. Cf. Clair Wilcox, *A Charter for World Trade* (New York, 1949), p. 70:

"Preferences have been opposed and customs unions favored, in principle, by the United States. This position may obviously be criticized as lacking in logical consistency. In preferential arrangements, discrimination against the outer world is partial; in customs unions, it is complete. But the distinction is none the less defensible. A customs union creates a wider trading area, removes obstacles to competition, makes possible a more economic allocation of resources, and thus operates to increase production and raise planes of living. A preferential system, on the other hand, retains internal barriers, obstructs economy in production, and restrains the growth of income and demand. It is set up for the purpose of conferring a privilege on producers within the system and imposing a handicap on external competitors. A customs union is conducive to the expansion of trade on a basis of multilateralism and non-discrimination; a preferential system is not."

There would seem to be little or nothing in what is said here about the *evils* of preference which is not potentially true also for customs unions; and equally little in what is said here about the *benefits* of customs unions which is acceptable further than as being potentially true if circumstances are right, and which, where true at all, is not also potentially true, if circumstances are right, of preferences.

as this way of putting it makes it sound.[7] On the legal side, the discussion of the bearing of the *degree* of preference on its compatibility with most-favored-nation obligations has sometimes led to the opposite conclusion, namely, that, on the principle a *majori ad minus,* if a customs union with its 100 per cent preferences is compatible with the most-favored-nation principle, still more must fractional preferences be compatible.[8] This seems plausible enough until it is realized that acceptance of this reasoning would have the practical consequence that 100 per cent preferences would be legal if incident to customs union and lesser preferences would be legal because greater ones were, so that *all* preferences would be legal. The moral is that on both the economic and legal side the problem is too complex to be settled by simple maxims.[9] A 50 per cent preference is economically either less desirable or more desirable than a 100 per cent preference according only as preference at all is under the circumstances desirable or undesirable.[10]

---

7. One is reminded of Dryden's "My wound is great because it is so small," and Saint-Evremond's rejoinder, "Then 'twould be greater, were it none at all."

8. Sandor von Matlekovits, *Die Zollpolitik der österreichisch-ungarischen Monarchie und des Deutschen Reiches scit 1868 und deren nächste Zukunft* (Leipzig, 1891).

9. The following illustration of the ambiguous working in practice of the *a majori ad minus* principle is not, it is hoped, wholly without relevance:

"It being made felony by an act of parliament to steal *horses,* it was doubted whether stealing *one horse only* was within the statute: in construction of penal law, the less number may not be included under the greater, but the reverse can never follow. Cf. the King of Prussia's error when he comments that, an English law prohibiting bigamy, a man accused of having five wives was acquitted, as not coming under the law." Daines Barrington, *Observations on the More Ancient Statutes,* 4th ed. (London, 1755), p. 547. (Italics in the original.)

10. It is to be remembered that administrative economies are here disregarded. If they were to be taken into account, a 100 per cent preference could be held more desirable than say a 99 per cent one on the ground that it made the economic wastes of customs formalities unnecessary—if it did—even though otherwise the smaller the preference the less objectionable it would be.

There is one ground only on which, aside from administrative considerations, it can consistently be held that preferences are economically bad and are increasingly bad as they approach 100 per cent, but that customs union is an economic blessing. Customs union, if it is complete, involves a cross-the-board removal of the duties between the members of the union; since the removal is non-selective by its very nature, the beneficial preferences are established along with the injurious ones, the trade-creating ones along with the trade-diverting ones. Preferential arrangements, on the other hand, can be, and usually are, selective, and it is possible, and in practice probable, that the preferences selected will be predominantly of the trade-diverting or injurious kind. But aside from possible administrative economies, cross-the-board 100 per cent preferences without customs union are economically as good—or as bad—as customs union.

From the free-trade point of view, that is, the point of view that movement in the direction of international specialization in production in accordance with comparative costs is economically desirable, there can be formulated in accordance with the preceding analysis a series of propositions as to the conditions which need to be met to justify the presumption that the establishment of a particular customs union will represent a movement toward free trade rather than away from it.

A customs union is more likely to operate in the free-trade direction, whether appraisal is in terms of its consequence for the customs union area alone or for the world as a whole:

(1) the larger the economic area of the customs union and therefore the greater the potential scope for internal division of labor;

(2) the lower the "average" tariff level on imports from outside the customs union area as compared to what that level would be in the absence of customs union;

(3) the greater the correspondence in kind of products of the range of high-cost industries as between the different parts of the customs union which were protected by tariffs in both of the member countries before customs union was established, i.e., the *less* the degree of complementarity—or the *greater* the degree of rivalry—of the member countries with respect to *protected* industries, prior to customs union;[11]

(4) the greater the differences in unit-costs for protected industries of the same kind as between the different parts of the customs union, and therefore the greater the economies to be derived from free trade with respect to these industries within the customs union area;

(5) the higher the tariff levels in potential export markets outside the customs union area with respect to commodities in whose production the member countries of the customs union would have a comparative advantage under free trade, and therefore the less the injury resulting from reducing the degree of specialization in production as between the customs union area and the outside world;

(6) the greater the range of protected industries for which an enlargement of the market would result in unit-costs lower than those at which the commodities concerned could be imported from outside the customs union area;

(7) the smaller the range of protected industries for which an enlargement of the market would not result in unit-costs lower than those at which the commodities concerned could be imported from outside the customs union area but which would nevertheless expand under customs union.

11. In the literature on customs union, it is almost invariably taken for granted that rivalry is a disadvantage and complementarity is an advantage in the formation of customs unions. See *infra*, pp. 73 ff., with reference to the Benelux and Franco-Italian projects.

Confident judgment as to what the over-all balance between these conflicting considerations would be, it should be obvious, cannot be made for customs unions in general and in the abstract, but must be confined to particular projects and be based on economic surveys thorough enough to justify reasonably reliable estimates as to the weights to be given in the particular circumstances to the respective elements in the problem. Customs unions are, from the free-trade point of view, neither necessarily good nor necessarily bad; the circumstances discussed above are the determining factors. As has been pointed out earlier, it would be easy to set up a hypothetical model where customs union would mean nothing economically except an intensification of uneconomic protection, an increase in the effectiveness of trade barriers as interferences with international division of labor. A universal customs union, on the other hand, would be the equivalent of universal free trade. Actual customs unions must fall somewhere between these two extremes.

The non-technical reader is again warned that this analysis not only takes for granted the validity—at least when only purely economic considerations are taken into account—of the argument for free trade from a cosmopolitan point of view, but that its results are much less favorable to customs union in general than the position taken by most free-trade economists who have discussed the issue.[12] One of the few exceptions is Lionel Robbins, whose formulation of the issue as here quoted is, in the opinion of the writer, excellent:

> ...The purpose of international division of labour is not merely to make possible the import of things which cannot

---

12. For conclusions, by economists sympathetic to free trade, more favorable to customs union, see especially: Gottfried von Haberler, *The Theory of International Trade* (London, 1936), pp. 383–91 and *idem*, "The Political Economy of Regional or

be produced on the spot; it is rather to permit the resources on the spot to be devoted wholly to the production of the things they are best fitted to produce, the remainder being procured from elsewhere.…

It follows, therefore, that the gain from regional regrouping or wider units of any kind is not a gain of greater self-sufficiency,

Continental Blocs," in Seymour E. Harris, *ed.*, *Postwar Economic Problems* (New York, 1943), especially pp. 330–34, and other writings of Haberler; John de Beers, "Tariff Aspects of a Federal Union," *Quarterly Journal of Economics* (1941), 49–92; and *Customs Unions*, 1947, pp. 75 ff., which follows Haberler's treatment closely and uncritically.

The more favorable conclusions with respect to customs unions reached by these writers are the consequence, mainly: (1) of failure to give consideration, or to give adequate consideration, to the effect of customs union in extending the area over which preexisting import duties exercise a protective effect; (2) of confusing the problem of the effect on location of production of customs union with the different, and for present purposes inconsequential, problem of the "incidence of import duties," or the location of impact of burden of payment of import duties actually collected; and (3) of applying the standard techniques of partial equilibrium analysis, traditionally applied to the analysis of the determination of prices of particular commodities taken one at a time, to foreign trade as a whole and to the tariff problem where its findings are either totally without significance or of totally indeterminable significance.

The present writer's own questioning in print of the usual arguments for customs union began in 1931: see "The Most-Favoured-Nation Clause," *Index*, VI (1931), p. 11. Haberler and de Beers have in the writings cited above found fault with the present writer's treatment as unduly critical of customs union, in part on the basis of reasoning of the type commented on in the preceding paragraph, and in part on the ground that the possibility of increased division of labor within the area of the customs union was denied or overlooked. In the few sentences devoted to the problem in the above-mentioned *Index* article, the writer asserted only the *possibility* that preferential duties would mean a greater diversion of trade from its free-trade pattern than uniform protection. He did not discuss the possibilities more favorable to customs union. Nor can he find in that article anything corresponding to the proposition attributed to him by de Beers, that an increase of imports must come from the same sources as under free trade, if there is to be gain. De Beers, however, cites a statement made by the present writer in 1933: "…if a regional agreement, preferential as between the countries within that region, is beneficial to both those countries, it must necessarily follow that had it been extended to the entire world but a gain of the abolition of so much self-sufficiency on the part of the areas which are thus amalgamated....[13]

... From the international point of view, the tariff union is not an advantage in itself. It is an advantage only in so far as, on balance, it conduces to more extensive division of labour. It is to be justified only by arguments which would justify still more its extension to all areas capable of entering into trade relationships.... No doubt if we could coax the rest of the world into free trade by a high tariff union against the produce of the Eskimos that would be, on balance, an international gain. But it would be inferior to an arrangement whereby the Eskimos were included. The only completely innocuous tariff union would be directed against the inaccessible produce of the moon.[14]

Another exception, however, seems to go further than is justified. R. G. Hawtrey writes as follows:

The most-favoured-nation clause has been criticised in that it prevented a relaxation of tariffs between adjacent countries, by which at any rate a beginning might have been made in the removal of obstacles to trade. A reduction of import

---

no substantial change would have resulted in the effect of the agreement." This *is* a faulty statement. It is taken from a non-verbatim report of an extemporaneous discussion which the writer had no opportunity to edit—and, may add, did not know until some years later to have been put into print. (See International Studies Conference, *The State and Economic Life* [Paris, 1934], p. 50). He makes no claim, however, to have been misreported, and is not now in a position to deny that it correctly represented the state of his thinking at that time.

13. Under customs union, there would he a decrease in the degree of self-sufficiency of, each member area, but an increase in the degree of self-sufficiency of the customs union area as a whole.

14. Lionel Robbins, *Economic Planning and International Order* (London, 1937), pp. 120–22.

duties by Belgium and Holland in favour of one another's products would have involved discrimination against other countries, such as Great Britain....

But to suppose that agreements of that kind would be a move towards free trade is a delusion. The preferential treatment that would have been given by Belgium and Holland to one another would have made their existing protective tariffs more exclusive against other countries. In fact the wider the extent of economic activity encircled by a tariff barrier of given height, the greater is its effect in excluding the goods of foreign producers. The break-up of the Austro-Hungarian Empire resulted in the creation of new frontiers, and the new tariff barriers obstructed trade between one succession State and another. But if the import duties had remained at the same level as before, the markets which the succession States lost in one another would have been more accessible than before to outside producers.[15]

Reduction of the extent of division of labor between the customs union area and the outside world is the major objective and would be a major consequence of most projected customs unions, and would be a consequence in some degree of *any* customs union with protective duties, unless the duties on imports from outside the customs union were drastically cut upon establishment of the union. But Hawtrey should not leave out of consideration the increase in the extent to which division of labor *within* the customs union area prevails as the result of customs union.

15. R. G. Hawtrey, *Economic Destiny* (London [1944]), pp. 135–36.

2. Customs Union and the "Terms of Trade"

There is a possibility, so far not mentioned, of economic benefit from a tariff to the tariff-levying country which countries may be able to exploit more effectively combined in customs union than if they operated as separate tariff areas. This benefit to the customs area, however, carries with it a corresponding injury to the outside world. A tariff does not merely divert consumption from imported to domestically produced commodities—this is, from the free-trade point of view, the economic disadvantage of a tariff for the tariff-levying country and one of its disadvantages for the rest of the world—but it also alters in favor of the tariff-levying country the rate at which its exports exchange for the imports which survive the tariff, or its "terms of trade," and within limits—which may be narrow and which can never be determined accurately—an improvement in the national "terms of trade" carries with it an increase in the national total benefit from trade. The greater the economic area of the tariff-levying unit, the greater is likely to be, other things being equal, the improvement in its terms of trade with the outside world resulting from its tariff.[16] A customs union, by increasing the extent of the territory which operates under a single tariff, thus tends to increase the efficacy of the tariff in improving the terms of trade of that area vis-à-vis the rest of the world.

The terms of trade of a customs area with the outside world can be influenced not only by its own tariff but by the tariffs of other countries. The higher the tariffs of other countries on its export products, the less favorable, other things equal, will be the terms of

---

16. The greater the economic area of the tariff unit, other things equal, the greater is likely to be the elasticity of its "reciprocal demand" for outside products and the less is likely to be the elasticity of the "reciprocal demand" of the outside world for its products, and consequently the greater the possibility of improvement in its terms of trade through unilateral manipulation of its tariff.

trade of a customs area with the outside world. But the level of foreign tariffs can be affected in some degree through tariff-bargaining, and the larger the bargaining unit the more effective its bargaining can be. The Balkans, for instance, could have secured better terms from Nazi Germany during the 1930's if they had bargained collectively with Germany rather than singly. This consideration has been an important element in fostering aspirations on the part of small countries for customs union. An abundance of historical evidence is available to show how significant has been its role in the movement for tariff unification, whether in the customs union form or in other forms, although not as a rule expounded in the sophisticated language of the "terms of trade" argument. A few historical instances will be cited.

The argument that under the Articles of Confederation, which left each state with its separate tariff, the United States was at a serious disadvantage in dealing with the commercial policy of Europe, and especially of Britain, was current among the founding fathers of the Republic and helped to create readiness on the part of the public to accept a closer federal union with tariff policy centrally controlled.[17]

In 1819–1820, France imposed heavy import duties on cattle. Baden, Württemberg, and some of the Swiss cantons which were hard hit by these duties thereupon negotiated an agreement whereby they were to engage jointly in retaliatory measures against France. The agreement was operative from 1822 to

17. Cf. the reports of the Committee on Commercial Policy, September 29, 1783, October 9, 1783, U. S. Continental Congress, *Journals of the Continental Congress 1774–1789*, W. C. Ford and Gaillard Hunt, *eds.* (Washington, 1904–37), XXV, 628–30, 661–64; message to President Washington by John Adams, Benjamin Franklin, and John Jay, from Paris, September 10, 1783, in *The Revolutionary Diplomatic Correspondence of the United States,* Francis Wharton, *ed.* (Washington, 1889), VI, 691; President Washington, August 22, 1785, as cited in O. L. Elliott, *The Tariff Controversy in the United States, 1789–1833* (Palo Alto, 1892), p. 46; the *Federalist* [1777–1778], No. XI; Joseph Story, *Commentaries on the Constitution,* Sections 1056–1073.

1824, when it lapsed because of the refusal of some of the Swiss cantons to give their adherence to the agreement and its consequent conflict with the customs provisions of the Swiss constitution, which prohibited separate action on the part of the cantons but provided no procedures for assuring concerted action. This demonstration that without more centralization of Swiss tariff authority no effective tariff-bargaining policy could be carried out helped in preparing the way for the Swiss Constitution of 1848, which put commercial policy under Federal Government control.[18]

The movement which sprang up in Europe toward the end of the nineteenth century for a "United States of Europe" arose in large part from the widespread belief that only through some form of European economic union could the "American menace" be satisfactorily dealt with. Often invoked in support of the movement was the doctrine, expounded especially by the German historical school of economists, that small countries are at a serious disadvantage in commercial competition with large countries. But the movement focused more particularly on the unfavorable impact of American competition and American tariff policy on disunited Europe. Many aspects of American-European commercial relations were pointed to as calling for concerted defensive action: effective American competition, first with European agriculture as overseas freight costs fell and the American West was opened up, next with European manufacturing industries as large-scale exports by the United States of manufactured products made their appearance; the high and ever-rising American tariff; the refusal of the United States to participate in the network of commercial treaties by which European

18. Cf. Joseph Litschi, "Das Retorsions-Konkordat vom Jahre 1822," *Zeitschrift für schweizerische Statistik*, XXVIII (1892), 1–22; Werner Bleuler, *Studien über Aussenhandel und Handelspolitik der Schweiz* (Zurich, 1929), pp. 35–36; *Mémoires et souvenirs de Augustin–Pyramus de Candolle* (Geneva, 1862), p. 313.

tariffs were being lowered or at least their rise checked; the adherence by the United States to the conditional interpretation of the most-favored-nation clause, whereby it was able to withhold from third countries what tariff concessions it did make to particular countries in "reciprocity" agreements, while claiming successfully the extension to imports from the United States of the concessions which European countries were making to each other;[19] the emergence of talk of customs union between the United States and Latin America; the export methods of the new but lusty American "trusts"; and so forth.[20]

Since until the advent of the Roosevelt Administration there was no improvement from the European point of view in American commercial policy, and the severity of American competition in world trade was, if anything, more pronounced than ever before, the interwar phase of the movement for European

19. For an explanation of how this was achieved, see Jacob Viner, "The Most-Favored-Nation Clause in American Commercial Treaties," *loc. cit.*, pp. 119–20.

20. No systematic study has apparently ever been made of the anti-American orientation of the movement for European union, 1880 and earlier to 1914. For comment by an American scholar, see George M. Fisk, "Continental Opinion regarding a Proposed Middle European Tariff Union," *Johns Hopkins University Studies in Historical and Political Science*, XX (1902), Nos. 11–12. The European source material is voluminous; the following items are representative: Henri Richelot, *L'Association douanière allemande* (Paris, 1843), p. 22; Michel Chevalier, "La guerre et la crise européenne," *Revue des deux mondes*, XXXVI² (1866), 758–85; Alexander Peez (an Austrian and a leader in the movement), *Die amerikanische Konkurrenz* (Leipzig, 1881), and "A propos de la situation douanière en Europe," *Revue d'économie politique*, V (1891), especially p. 138; Auguste Oncken, "L'Article onze du Traité de Paix de Franefort." *ibid.*, p. 602; Edmond Théry, *Europe et Etats-Unis d'Amérique* (Paris, 1899), the preface by Marcel Dubois; Ernst von Halle, "Das Interesse Deutschlands an der amerikanischer Präsidentenwahl des Jahres 1896," *Jahrbuch für Gesetzgebung, Verwaltung und Volkswirtschaft* ("Schmoller's *Jahrbuch*"), New Series, XX (1896), 263–96; Gaston Domerque, "Le péril américain," *La réforme économique,* May 26, 1901, February 2, 1902, June 15, 1902, etc.; Richard Calwer, *Die Meistbegüstigung der Vereinigten Staaten von Nordamerika* (Berlin, 1902); Rudolf Kobatsch, *La politique économique internationale* (Paris, 1913), pp. 375–89. Cf. also L. Bosc, *op. cit.*, pp. 428–86.

union still retained, if less pronouncedly and less frankly than before, a distinctly anti-American orientation.[21]

3. Administrative Economies of Customs Union

(a) The Removal of Internal Tariff Walls

The burdens on trade of a customs tariff, and its hindrances to trade, arise not only from the actual levy of duties—which for all the countries concerned taken in the aggregate are, of course, exactly offset, in monetary terms at least, by the revenues accruing to the levying government—but also from the costs involved, for exporter and importer, in meeting the customs regulations, and the costs involved, for the tariff-levying government, in administering the customs machinery. These costs are often, in fact, more important than the duties themselves as hindrances to trade,[22] so that if the duties were lowered to a nominal level but the customs administrative code remained as before, the tariff could still constitute an important restriction on trade. But the United States is an outstanding offender in this respect. In

21. See, e.g., the report of a speech in Vienna in 1926 by Reichstag President Loebe in M. Margaret Ball, *Post-War German-Austrian Relations: The Anschluss Movement, 1918–1936* (Stanford University, 1937), p. 72, and the comment of *Izvestia,* as reported in Kathryn W. Davis, *The Soviets at Geneva* (Geneva, 1934), p. 227, note, on Briand's plan for European union, as primarily a European defense against "American capitalist aggression on the one hand and Bolshevist revolutionary aggressiveness on the other."

22. Cf. *Monthly Review, The Bank of Nova Seotia,* New Series, No. 26, Toronto, July, 1948: "Nor are the barriers against imports into the United States a matter of tariff rates alone. Canadian exporters have long maintained that the difficulties connected with U. S. customs procedures, the complexity of the regulations, and the delays and uncertainties arising out of their administration are in some cases an even greater hindrance to trade than the tariff rates themselves." See also R. Elberton Smith, *Customs Valuation in the United States* (Chicago, 1948).

the case of most other tariffs, their removal would not involve comparable administrative economies.

If a customs union were "complete" or "perfect," so that the tariff wall were completely removed between its members, this would constitute therefore an important relaxation of trade barriers between members of the union aside from the removal of the duties themselves as well as a reduction of administrative expense to the governments of the member countries, since the frontier—or frontiers—between them would no longer have to be watched for customs purposes.[23] The more important economically, and the longer or more difficult to watch, the removed tariff frontier was, the more important per unit volume of trade would be the administrative economies resulting from its removal. Given the economic area of the customs union, the larger also the number of tariff frontiers eliminated as a result of the formation of the union, the greater, other things equal, would be the administrative economies resulting therefrom per unit volume of trade. Customs union, however, even if complete, results in the full elimination for administrative purposes of tariff frontiers only if and to the extent that the territories of the members of the union are contiguous territories. Even if no third country intervenes between two members of a customs union, the existence between them of "high seas" is sufficient to cut down, perhaps drastically, the administrative economies of customs union. "The sea, it is said, unites and does not separate, which is true in a sense, but is not true for the purpose of a Zollverein."[24] Customs unions, actual or projected, however, appear invariably to include only contiguous territory.[25]

---

23. This assumes that import duties are the only deliberate trade barriers, or that quantitative restrictions, etc., are also removed.

24. Sir Robert Giffen, *Economic Inquiries and Studies* (London, 1904), II, 393.

25. If the relations of metropolitan France with those of its colonies which are "assimilated" to France for tariff purposes, and the relations of the United States

It would be a mistake, however, to assume that the administrative changes consequent upon customs union all involve economies. Where the administration of the customs union is not entrusted wholly to one of the members of the union, there are additional burdens of negotiation, of coordination of codes, and of mutual supervision which may substantially reduce the net economies as well as give rise to political frictions. The necessity of coordination and of mutual supervision may force a standardization and simplification of duties which on other grounds may be undesirable. It has been suggested, for instance, that the number of countries which had a right to participate in the administration of the German Zollverein made it necessary to confine the Zollverein tariff mainly to specific duties, since the administrative task of assuring that ad valorem duties would be uniformly interpreted and applied at all the frontiers of the Zollverein would have been an almost insuperable one.[26]

Where excise taxes are important and customs union does not carry with it standardization of excise taxes throughout the territory of the union, the "tariff wall" between the members of the union, moreover, cannot wholly be removed, since otherwise the excise tax systems would be undermined by the flow of commodities affected from the untaxed, or low tax, areas to the tax, or higher tax, areas. In the earlier days of customs unions, this was a major problem in the negotiation and administration of such unions, since excise taxes were then relatively more important than they are today as sources of government revenue, and the texts of earlier customs union treaties show how much attention had to be given to this problem, and how complex were the administrative measures required to deal with it. The complexity

with Puerto Rico may be taken to constitute "customs union," they provide illustrative instances of the administrative economics of customs union being only partially available because of the existence of high seas between the members of the union.

26. W. O. Henderson, *op. cit.*, p. 278.

of the problem may, in fact, have been a significant factor in preventing customs union agreements from being reached.[27] Even today, moreover, especially given the revival of resort on a large scale to indirect taxation as a source of government revenue, a good deal of the possible administrative economy of customs union would be likely to be lost if the establishment of uniformity of excise taxes did not accompany the formation of the customs union.

It may be objected that American experience demonstrates that this is not an important problem, since the absence of tariff walls between the States has proved to be consistent with the levy by the States of non-uniform excise taxes. But state excise taxes in the United States, though growing in range and severity, are still levied as a rule only on a very limited range of commodities and at very moderate rates. They have not been unassociated, moreover, with the development of troublesome and irritating equivalents of state tariff walls, which have rightly become a matter of growing concern.[28]

Furthermore, the growth under "central planning" of disguised inflation, non-equilibrium exchange rates, price controls, subsidies, and so forth, makes it impossible today completely to remove trade barriers unless economic union is carried far beyond the customs union stage. But this applies, probably with

---

27. Cf. G. de Molinari, "Union douanière de l'Europe," *Journal des économistes,* 4th Series, 2d year, V (1879), pp. 314–15: "The most serious difficulty, and we can even say the sole genuinely serious difficulty which the formation of an international *Zollverein* will face, rests in the standardization of excise régimes. This difficulty has not yet been entirely overcome in Germany, where there has not been achieved a uniform tax on beer and spirits, which has made necessary the maintenance of a frontier (*ligne*) for the protection of the excises between the North and the South."

28. Cf. Frederick E. Melder, *State and Local Barriers to Interstate Commerce in the United States* (Orono, Maine, 1937), and U. S. Department of Commerce, Bureau of Foreign and Domestic Commerce, *Bibliography of Barriers to Trade between States* (Washington, 1942).

greater force, to general as well as to preferential removals of trade barriers.[29]

(b) The Elimination of Taxes on Goods in Transit

One type of economy associated with customs union, namely, the elimination of transit duties, and of ordinary import duties on goods in transit, for members of the union, which was once of great importance, is now of little or no significance. In the early part of the nineteenth century, when transportation costs were high and the importance of using the lowest-cost route therefore great, heavy transit duties were common. Countries in a favorable geographical position exploited to the full the opportunity to levy toll on commerce crossing their territories. The exemption from transit duties on commerce crossing Prussian territory was a major inducement which Prussia could offer other German states to enter into customs union with her since Prussian territory lay astride all the major routes for commerce between and through the German states to the north and the southern German states.[30]

Collection of duties on imported goods in transit to a third state, in conjunction with discriminatory railway rates, played an

---

29. Cf. Etienne Mantoux, *The Carthaginian Peace* (New York, 1946), p. 189: "whatever increases the economic significance of the State will inevitably increase the economic significance of frontiers. How, in the present trend of economic policy, it is possible to make insignificant frontiers coexist with all-pervading states is utterly beyond the present writer's powers of imagination."

30. A petition for customs union submitted in 1818 by a German group under the chairmanship of Friedrich List contains the following passage:

"To make a commercial shipment from Hamburg to Austria and from Berlin to Switzerland, one must cross ten states, study ten sets of customs regulations pay six different transit duties. He who has the misfortune to reside at a frontier where three or four states touch each other, passes his entire life bickering with customs officials: he has not got a fatherland." Cited in J. Pentmann, *Dic Zolluniousidce und three Wandlungen* (1917), p. 9.

especially important role in the history of the movement toward customs union in South Africa. The Transvaal and the Orange Free State—later the Orange River Colony—were shut off from direct access to the sea to the south by Cape Colony and Natal and elsewhere by absence of railroads or even roads. The coastal colonies exploited their geographical position to the fullest extent which their rivalry with each other permitted by levying their full import duties on imports from outside Africa passing to the interior republics through their territory and also by charging heavier rates for transportation on their railways of commodities coming from overseas than for competing commodities of their own production.[31] At one time the Transvaal, under Oom Paul Kruger, sought escape from these exactions by building a railroad to Delagoa Bay in Portuguese East Africa and, to force

Cf. also the dispatch to the Foreign Office from the British envoy to the German Diet, December, 1834, cited in Herbert C. F. Bell, *Lord Palmerston* (London, 1936), I, 159, from the British Foreign Office archives: "...hemmed in by a line of Custom Houses all round the Gates of the Town, its [Frankfort's] commercial intercourse with the interior of Germany was greatly harassed and restricted....its commerce and trade had already fallen off considerably, and...great apprehensions were entertained that its Fairs would be irretrievably injured unless the Union with Prussia was speedily effected;...the British Houses...funding their old customers deterred from frequenting the Fairs and their buyers diminish, had themselves become the advocates of the Union with Prussia...."

31. The treatment of sugar by Natal was a notorious example. Cf. Transvaal, *Report of the Customs & Industries Commission* (Pretoria, 1908), p. 5: "Natal sugar is carried at a very much lower rate than sugar imported from oversea, the result being that the further inland the sugar travels the higher the protection afforded against the oversea traffic. In consequence of this and of the fact that the production of sugar in Natal is far below the consumption of the Union, the bulk of the sugar produced is sent inland to the Transvaal, Orange River and Cape Colonies, while Natal very largely imports sugar from oversea for its own consumption; on these importations the Natal Government collects and retains duties amounting to a considerable sum, to a large proportion of which the Transvaal Government is fairly entitled." Cf. also the Memorandum prepared by the Earl of Selborne, January, 1907, in A. P. Newton, ed., *Select Documents relating to the Unification of South Africa* (London, 1924), II, 418. This was *after* customs union was established, and was possible because the customs union agreement left to each territory, with some exceptions, the customs duties collected within that territory.

traffic from overseas to take the Delagoa Bay route, imposed heavy freight rates on the portion of the Cape-to-Johannesburg railroad which lay within Transvaal territory. The Orange Free State did not have even this alternative available, and its only defense was in its ability to thwart the railway-building plans of the coastal colonies by excluding their lines from its territory. "But much as he [President Brand of the Free State] wanted the money, he wanted the railways more. The colonies knew it and continued to rob the republic."[32]

It might be supposed that these were just the types of evil in commercial relations for which customs union would provide an effective remedy. But when the South African Customs Union Conventions of 1903 and 1906 were negotiated, the former Boer republics, defeated in war, had not yet been given responsible government, and were represented at the negotiations by British officials. It was not until the establishment of political union between the four colonies in 1910 that the allocation of customs revenues and the structure of railway rates ceased to be patently unfair to the Transvaal and the Orange Free State.[33]

32. Jean Van der Poel, *Railway and Customs Policies in South Africa 1885–1910* (London, 1933), pp. 11–12.

33. In addition to the references given above, A. J. Bruwer, *Protection in South Africa* (Stellenbosch, 1923), a University of Pennsylvania doctoral dissertation, can be profitably consulted. There is an extensive bibliography in Bruwer of literature published up to 1921.

The fear that the United States would resume the collection of customs duties on traffic from Europe to the Province of Canada (i.e., Ontario and Quebec) was an important contributory factor to the formation of the Canadian Confederation. An Act of Congress of 1845 provided for drawbacks of customs duties on through traffic to Canada across American territory and other legislation granted such traffic the privilege of transit in bond without payment of duties. It was feared in Canada that, with the Southern states for the time being deprived of a voice in Congress and the North aggressive because of anti-British animosity and annexationist ambitions, these privileges would be withdrawn. Canadian Confederation would make

For European countries, the revolution in transportation which occurred in the nineteenth century resulted in shippers as a rule not being confined to single practicable routes and therefore deprived countries of the power of exacting as monopolists high tolls on transit trade, and, instead, caused them to eliminate transit duties and to compete for transit traffic by improving traffic facilities, lowering freight rates on railroads, and reducing administrative obstructions to economical transportation. By the end of the century transit duties had almost wholly disappeared in Europe. They were outlawed for signatory countries by the Covenant of the League of Nations, and by the Barcelona Conference on Communications and Transit of 1921. Article 33 of the Havana Charter reproduces and strengthens the provisions for freedom of transit of the Barcelona Conference.

The elimination of transit duties is, indeed, the only significant nineteenth-century reform in the field of commercial policy which is surviving unimpaired in the twentieth century; to economic developments which make almost any country's departure from freedom of transit patently unprofitable to it, rather than to international diplomacy, the progress of economic enlightenment, or the will to international economic cooperation, belongs the credit. The improvement of transportation facilities which, by opening up the possibility of competition between alternative routes for the transit business, led to the elimination of transit duties, by intensifying competition between countries also led to a general raising of tariffs.[34] For the customs union question

possible construction of a railway route to the Atlantic wholly in Canadian territory. Cf. Donald C. Masters, *The Reciprocity Treaty of 1854* (London, 1937), p. 229, and R. G. Trotter, *Canadian Federation* (Toronto, 1924), pp. 126 ff. In this case, the duties on transit trade levied by one state operated to foster unification of *other* states.

34. Cf. G. de Molinari, "Union douanière le l'Europe centrale," *loc. cit.,* p. 318: "Is it not absurd to pay at the same time engineers to facilitate the transport of persons and merchandise, and customs officers to make it more difficult?"

the significance of this development is that the formation of customs unions no longer has a major contribution to make to the freeing of transit trade from artificial burdens.

4. Revenue Duties

In the discussion so far, the question of revenue duties has not been dealt with. If the revenue yield of the tariff as a whole is substantial for one or more of the countries entering into customs union, this will complicate the problem of negotiation of the union. If the revenue yield of the customs union tariff is substantial, there will be the problem of how to allocate these revenues between the members. These problems will be considered in a subsequent section.

In so far as the effect of the formation of customs unions on international specialization in production is concerned, the existence of revenue duties raises no new question of principle. It is not easy sharply to distinguish between revenue duties and protective duties. For present purposes, revenue duties may be regarded as those duties productive of revenue which do not act as effective stimulus to the domestic production of commodities *similar* to those paying the duties. Even such duties, however, if they are not offset by general excises on commodities of domestic production, operate to increase the proportion of aggregate domestic consumption which is directed toward domestically produced commodities. The only differences, then, between revenue duties and protective duties which are significant for present

In a memorandum of 1815 to the Government of the Canton of Geneva, Sismondi argued that the widened range of transportation routes which bad become available made it impracticable for Geneva to levy transit duties. See Jean R. De Salis, *Sismondi 1775–1842: Lettres et documents inédits* (Paris, 1932), p. 23.

purposes is that revenue duties have only a generalized protective effect, whereas protective duties have both this generalized effect and a specific effect in stimulating the domestic production of commodities similar to those subject to the protective duty, with the consequence that protective duties tend to he more effective than revenue duties as restraints on importation. Revenue duties can be regarded therefore as the equivalent of protective duties of slight effectiveness, or a high revenue duty may be regarded as the equivalent of a moderate protective duty, for present purposes.

The existence of revenue duties, therefore, does not make it necessary to change in any respect the conclusions as to the effect of customs union on international specialization reached on the basis of the assumption that there were no revenue duties. If a customs union should be established. however, between two countries which before had only revenue duties and if all the duties levied by the customs union continue to operate as "pure" revenue duties, the appraisal of the customs union would turn chiefly on its administrative economics or inconveniences, or on political aspects, and the foregoing analysis would be largely irrelevant for it. Some of the intercolonial customs unions are wholly or substantially in this category.[35]

5. The "Level" of the Customs Union Tariff

Whatever tendency the formation of a customs union may have to lessen the extent of international specialization, the lower the

---

35. The fear that customs union would result in loss of revenues has sometimes operated for both the prospective members as a factor against proceeding with customs union negotiations. It is of course a probable result where the prospective members have a large volume of dutiable trade with each other before customs union, and also where customs union will divert a large amount of import trade from outside countries to member countries.

rates of duty in the customs union tariff, the less effect of this kind, other things equal, will it have.

Resolutions in favor of customs union often have a proviso that the customs union tariff should not be "higher" than the tariffs of the member countries prior to the formation of the union. The Havana Charter (Article 44, paragraph 2) sanctions the formation of customs union without the requirement of prior approval by the International Trade Organization provided the duties (and other restrictions) on imports into the union are "not on the whole...higher or more restrictive than the general incidence" of the duties (and other restrictions) on imports of the member countries prior to the formation of such union. What meaning can be given to such provisos?

There is no way in which the "height" of a tariff as an index of its restrictive effect can be even approximately measured, or, for that matter, even defined with any degree of *significant* precision.[36] It is possible to say that some proposed methods of measurement are less illogical than others. It may be possible to say, after careful examination and in the light of extensive background information, that one tariff is clearly higher than another. But it is scarcely possible to find a way of measuring the relative height in quantitative terms of two tariffs. An identical tariff might be high for one country or at one time and low for another country or at another time.

In the case of a customs union, if its tariff is made up of the highest rates on each class of imports previously levied by either (or any) of the member countries—and still more if the customs union rates are set even higher than this—the new tariff is clearly "more restrictive" of imports from outside the union

---

36. Cf. Jacob Viner, "The Measurement of the 'Height' of Tariff Levels," Joint Committee, Carnegie Endowment–International Chamber of Commerce, *The Improvement of Commercial Relations between Nations* (Paris, 1936), pp. 58–68.

than were the previous tariffs. But even if the new tariff is made up of the *lowest* rates previously levied by either (or any) of the member countries on each class of imports dutiable in both, it may still be "more restrictive" in fact, whether or not in the intent of the Havana Charter provision, than the previous tariffs, because customs union operates to convert revenue duties to protective duties.[37] Some part of an old higher rate may have been ineffective for the country levying it because even a lower rate would have been completely prohibitive of imports, while the lower rate of the other country may previously have been low enough to permit imports from third countries, whereas now, because of preferential treatment of imports from the other member country, it operates to exclude imports from third countries completely, or at least more completely than before. Thus a customs union tariff which, in the interpretations commonly given to "level of tariff," is lower than the average level of the previous tariffs of the member countries, and even one which is lower than either (or any) of these tariffs, may still be "more

---

37. There is little likelihood that the Havana Charter provision will be given so exacting an interpretation. In the Benelux customs union, the new level of duties is commonly said to be about half-way between the (lower) rates of the previous Netherlands tariff and the (higher) rates of the previous Belgium-Luxemburg tariff, although this is true only in a limited sense. The Dutch tariff of 1934 comprised only 160 dutiable classes of items, and all unenumerated articles were exempt from duty. The Belgian tariff listed many more dutiable articles, and moreover made subject to duty all items not expressly exempted. In the Benelux tariff it is only on items which were common to the two tariffs that the new rates are half-way between the previous Netherlands and the previous Belgium-Luxemburg tariff rates, and all items not expressly exempted are made dutiable. The new tariff is therefore much closer to the previous higher Belgian tariff than to the previous Netherlands tariff. The relations between the old and the new tariffs are in fact more complicated than this indicates, because of changes in classification, the substitution of ad valorem for specific duties, and other factors. Examination of the old and the new tariffs by an American expert has resulted in the conclusion that "it may be stated generally that the Benelux Tariff is more protectionist than the Netherlands tariff, and that it apparently is not less protectionist than the Belgo-Luxembourg tariff." W. Buchdahl, "The New 'Benelux' Union–Western Europe Tariff Pattern?" U. S. Department of

restrictive" of imports into the customs union territory from outside that territory than were the previous tariffs of the member countries. But customs union tariffs have not typically been "low" even in these senses of the term.

6. Increased Tariff Protection as the Major Economic Objective of Customs Unions

The tariff unification movement, in the nineteenth century and since, in so far as it culminated in actual arrangements or at least reached the stage of serious negotiations on an official basis, was primarily a movement to make high protection feasible and effective for limited areas going beyond the frontiers of single states, and to promote self-sufficiency for these larger areas because self-sufficiency for single states was clearly impracticable or too costly; it was not a movement to promote the international division of labor. It would be exceedingly difficult to demonstrate this, partly because clear definition and statement of objectives is often not essential for nor even helpful to effective negotiation, partly because there were obvious and weighty reasons why it would have been inexpedient to attract attention to this phase of the movement. There is nevertheless no lack of circumstantial evidence to support this interpretation. This objective becomes explicit here and there in the literature of advocacy of customs

Commerce, *Foreign Commerce Weekly,* October 11, 1947, pp. 3–5, 32. Since the increase in protection is not overt and unambiguous, however, there has been no suggestion from any quarter that this involves any conflict with the Havana Charter. An American Congressional Subcommittee has commented: "This procedure of establishing new common tariffs at, roughly, the average of the old tariffs is in accordance with the draft charter of the International Trade Organization." U. S. Congress, House Select Committee on Foreign Aid, Subcommittee on France and the Low Countries, Preliminary Report Twenty-Four, *The Belgian-Luxemburg-Netherlands Customs and Economic Union* (1948), p. 2.

unions,[38] and underlies all of the nineteenth-century literature favoring European Economic Union as a means of coping with American competition. It reveals itself in the special provisions in customs union agreements intended to check the intensification of competition between the member areas which would otherwise result from the arrangement.[39] The aversion to opening their markets to the competition from each other's industries has been the chief factor economic in character which was responsible for so few customs unions actually being consummated when so many projects were launched.

Where of two potential members of a customs union one is predominantly free-trade or low-tariff in interest and sentiment while the other is protectionist and provides only a negligible market for the staple exports of the first, the low-tariff territory will not voluntarily enter into the union except as part of a political union and for predominantly political reasons, and even after it has entered it is likely to find the union economically irksome because the chief economic consequence of the union is to make its territory an additional field of operation for the tariff protection of its partner's industries. Such has been largely the case for the Transvaal and the Orange River Colony vis-à-vis the South African Customs Union, for the Prairie Provinces of Canada vis-à-vis the Canadian Confederation, for Western Australia in relation to the Australian Commonwealth. Such was also the

---

38. Cf. especially Henry Masson, "Les unions douanières," an extract from the Report of the Congrès International d'Expansion Economique Mondiale, held at Mons, Belgium, 1905.

39. The role of the "Zwischenzoll" in the history of the Austro-Hungarian Customs Union is especially pertinent here. The major difficulty in keeping the customs union intact arose out of the insistence of the members, and especially of Hungary, that the customs union should not remove the barriers to competition between the members. Cf. Rudolf Sieghart, *Zolltrennung und Zolleinheit: Die Geschichte der österreichisch ungarischen Zwischenzoll-linie* (Vienna, 1915); Ivor L. Evans, "Economic Aspects of Dualism in Austria-Hungary," *The Slavonic Review*, VI (1927–28), 529–42;

case for the Southern States in relation to the American Federal Union prior to the industrialization of the South. Such was for a time at least the case with respect to the Swiss Federal Union.[40] It was largely true also in the history of the German Zollverein, although Prussia for a variety of reasons—partial conversion to free-trade views, willingness to make economic concessions in order to establish a base for eventual political unification, readiness to keep the Zollverein tariff low in order to lessen Austrian determination to obtain entrance to it—for a time supported a low-tariff policy for the Zollverein.

The Tanganyika-Kenya Customs Union provides a striking instance where a territory was brought into a customs union by external authority in order to provide an expanded field for the tariff protection of the industries of another territory.[41] Tanganyika, captured by the British from the Germans in World War I, is a mandate territory. The British first introduced a

Louis Eisenmann, *Le compromis austro-hongrois de 1867: étude sur le dualisme* (Paris, 1904); Joseph Grunzel, *Handeispolitik und Ausgleich in Österreich-Ungarn* (Vienna, 1912), especially pp. 115, 224, 237. For the manipulation of railway rates within Austria-Hungary, as a substitute for internal import duties, see Ivor Evans, *op. cit.*, p. 539.

40. Cf. Werner Bleuler, *Studien über Aussenhandel und Handelspolitik der Schwviz* (Zurich, 1929), p. 37, with reference to the situation in Switzerland in the 1830's:

"These free-trade traditions, in conjunction with the hereditary federalist views were an obstacle to the tariff unification of the land; for the economic controversy, Free Trade versus Protection, stood in the then prevailing opinion and circumstances in close connection with the political issue Federalism versus Centralization. The attitude was widespread that a unified Swiss tariff policy would at the same time be a protectionist one. People said to themselves, a unification of the customs would work in two ways: first it would reduce the political autonomy of the Cantons and would make openings for centralizing activities in other spheres, and second it would have the consequence that they would be gradually drawn into the channel of protectionist politics. Thus both the convinced Free traders and the extreme Federalists were opposed to the unification movement."

41. The relation of the Transvaal and the Orange River Colony to the South African Customs Union provides an analogous earlier instance. See *supra*, pp. 62 ff.

new tariff in Tanganyika in 1921, higher than the German one, and then in 1923 changed the tariff again, making it identical with the still higher tariff of the Kenya-Uganda customs union, while abolishing the customs barriers between the three territories, all in preparation for full customs union. In 1927 full customs union was established, despite questioning from the British Governor of Tanganyika as to its suitability to the mandate's economic interests. The customs union operated to create a protected market in Tanganyika for the produce of the small colony of British planters in Kenya, for whose welfare the British Government has shown a constant and marked solicitude. To reinforce the tariff in providing a preferential market for Kenya produce in Tanganyika, a system of preferential rates on the railways, under which commodities of external origin paid higher rates than customs-union produce, also was introduced. After an investigation of the operation of the customs union on behalf of the British Colonial Office, Sir Sydney Armitage-Smith, an economist of repute and an objective civil servant, reached the conclusion that "Tanganyika should take steps forthwith to levy customs import duty at the same rates on foodstuffs imported from Kenya and Uganda as those chargeable on foodstuffs imported from foreign parts, and should cease to deplete her revenue and impoverish her citizens by protecting the products of her neighbours."[42]

The progressive contraction in range of application and decline in efficacy of the most-favored-nation clause have

---

42. "Report by Sir Sydney Armitage-Smith, on a Financial Mission to Tanganyika, 26th September, 1932. Presented by the Secretary of State for the Colonies to Parliament, October, 1932." British Parliamentary Papers, Cmd. 4182, 1932, p. 25. See also Charlotte Leubuscher, *Tanganyika Territory: A Study of Economic Policy under Mandate* (London, 1944), pp. 101–20, for an excellent treatment of this problem. Miss Leubuscher criticizes the League of Nations Mandates Commission for not giving sufficient attention to the economic effects of the customs union.

increased the range of special commercial arrangements which permit concerted action to restrict imports from countries outside the arrangement without involving either the removal of the barriers to competition between the members or sharp conflict with most-favored-nation obligations to third countries. A significant illustration is provided by the Argentine-Brazil commercial treaty of November, 1941, and the Argentine-Chile trade agreement of August, 1943, both designated as providing a base for eventual customs union, and both clearly and frankly designed to extend the effective area of protection from external competition of the industries of the participant countries without increasing the competition between the industries of the two countries. The crucial provisions in the Argentine-Brazil treaty are the following:

ARTICLE I.—1. The High Contracting Parties undertake to promote, stimulate and facilitate the installation in their respective countries of industrial and agricultural and livestock activities as yet not in existence in either of the two, mutually undertaking:

(*a*) Not to collect import duties during a period of ten years from the date of the entry into force of this Treaty on the products of such new activities;

. . . .

(*c*) To arrive at protective measures with respect to competition by similar products from other sources when these can be classed as "dumping."

2. For the purposes of this Treaty industrial and agricultural and livestock activities described as non-existent are those not installed in either of the two countries at the date of the signature of this Treaty.

3. In order to enjoy the advantages provided for herein, the articles not included in the list referred to in Article IV will be considered not produced in either of the two countries.

ARTICLE II. With respect to the articles produced in one of the two countries or which are of little economic importance in one of them the High Contracting Parties undertake not to apply, during a period of ten years from the date of entry into force of this Treaty, duties of a protectionist nature on imports, but rather, on the contrary, to grant them special preference, not to be extended to other suppliers.

. . . .

ARTICLE III. The High Contracting Powers mutually agree to extend the benefits of the preceding Article to those products of economic importance customs tariffs on which may be gradually reduced or eliminated without affecting present production or national economy.

ARTICLE IV. In order to put into effect the preceding provisions, the High Contracting Parties undertake to draw up, within a term of six months from the date of the signature of this Treaty, a list of all the articles already produced in each country, indicating the economic importance of such production, that is to say: the number of factories, capital invested, value and volume of present production, maximum capacity of production, total consumption of such products in the country, and other facts of interest for the study of the form in which free trade may be established between the two countries without affecting existing production and national economy.

ARTICLE VIII. The High Contracting Parties will appoint, once the lists referred to in Article IV have been exchanged, the organisms in charge of putting into practice the provisions of the present Treaty.[43]

The Argentine-Chile treaty was similar in character. The essential feature of both treaties was that they provided for removal or relaxation of trade barriers on a preferential basis only for such commodities as involved little or no competition between themselves, and to effectuate this, provided for the non-competitive development of new industries. Later, apparently, Chile closed with Brazil an agreement by which Brazil undertook not to establish a domestic nitrate industry, and with the Argentine an agreement by which the Argentine obligated itself for a minimum period of ten years to use only Chilean nitrates[44]—developments in the same direction.

The development of quantitative restrictions on imports has facilitated the removal of tariff barriers between pairs of countries without involving the opening of each other's territory to full competition from the industries of the other. The Benelux Customs Union Agreement, signed at London September 5, 1944, which as revised by the Hague Protocol of March 14, 1947, came into operation on January 1, 1948, provided for removal of tariff duties between the members and a common tariff against imports from the outside world, but left intact, except as subsequently to be altered by mutual agreement, the whole machinery of import quotas, import licenses, special license dues and administrative fees, and subsidies, both with respect to imports from outside the Union and with respect to the intra-Union trade. These devices can, in principle, be so operated as to make

43. *Customs Unions*, 1947, pp. 92–93. The Spanish text corresponding to the words "special preference" in Article II reads: *"favores especiales de países limitrofes."* *Informaciones argentinas*, December 15, 1941, p. 3.

44. *New York Times*, April 24, 1943, dispatch from Santiago.

an economic union confined to ordinary tariffs operate in such a way as to involve no over-all relaxation in the effective barriers to competition between the industries of the member countries.

In the planning for further economic unification now in process, distinction is being made between "complementary," "parallel," and potentially or actually "rival" industries, and it seems clear from press reports that it is intended on both sides to provide, at least for a lengthy transition period, obstacles to free competition within the customs union area of rival industries.

For an important list of industries,[45] the governments must consult in the Council of the Economic Union before they sanction expansion. Likewise, there is a Committee for Industrial Development in which representatives of the three governments sit with delegates of trade organizations to deal with the same problem. There will also be, on a third level, reliance on government-sanctioned cartel agreements to restrain competition within the customs-union area between rival national industries.[46]

The negotiations for a Franco-Italian Customs Union now in progress are following similar lines. The First Joint Commission, acting in accordance with instructions received in September, 1947, in its Report of December 22, 1947, stated in unexceptional if vague terms the function of a customs union:

> The purpose of a customs union is essentially to permit, by virtue of the establishment of a more extensive economic

---

45. Window glass, carbonic acid, copper sulphate, explosives, coal and coke, sodium carbonate, steel, ball-bearings, steel balls, chains, plywood, furniture, strawboard, cement, rubber manufactures, sugar manufactures, rice-hulling, vegetable oils, flour-milling, beer, nitrogen.

46. See "Benelux...An Example of Unity in a Divided World," *Rotterdamsche Bank Quarterly Review,* 1947, No. 4, pp. 5–42, and "Benelux and Industrial Development," *Amsterdamsche Bank Quarterly Review,* No. 80, April, 1948, p. 15.

territory, a division of labor more developed, better adapted to the existing natural and economic conditions, and consequently a more abundant and lower-cost production destined for a greater market.[47]

As the Report proceeds to examine particular products, however, it finds difficulties everywhere except where the economies of the two countries are "complementary" (that is, where customs union would operate to extend the area of effective protection against competition from outside); and where industries are parallel or are rival, it emphasizes the need for regulation and understandings for coordinated export of their products and for coordinated import of their raw materials, to avoid competition in trade with the outside world. To avoid "dangerous competition" *within* the Union, allocation of capital and raw materials, industrial agreements, and other unspecified measures are suggested, but the general drift of the discussion of this problem, though vague at crucial points, indicates that full economic unification of the area, with competition between the areas as free— or as restricted—as within each area, is the long-run goal.[48]

The Second Joint Commission, set up in June, 1948, has recently submitted its report, and negotiations are proceeding toward an eventual customs union on the basis of the procedures recommended by this report. Here also the problem of "rival" industries receives emphasis. An interim period is contemplated when competition between the industries of the two countries will be restricted by compensatory taxes in the country of lower costs, by cartel agreements, and by regulated specialization in types of products. For the long run, however, the issue of rival

47. Commission Mixte Franco-Italienne pour l'Etude d'une Union Douanière entre la France et l'Italie, *Rapport final* (Paris; Imprimerie Nationale, 1948), p. 6.

48. *Ibid.,* pp. 48–49.

industries is more frankly faced and competition between them within the Union accepted as unavoidable:

> Certainly the Customs Union between France and Italy will derive its chief interest from the competition which this Union will establish between the two economies, which are only, as is known, very partially complementary. It is to be expected that there will result from this competition a more developed specialization, either because each country extends its production of those commodities for which it is better situated naturally, or because within the same category of products the two countries agree to specialize on specified types.[49]

7. Cartels in Relation to Customs Unions

There has long been an association of sorts between the tariff union idea and the international cartel idea as remedies through international cooperation for the problems arising in European countries from "excessive competition" in their markets from other countries, usually the United States.[50] This association has perhaps most often taken the form of rivalry, but frequently enough the two ideas became combined to constitute joint elements in a single plan for lessening the severity of international competition. Beginning with the preparatory work for the Geneva Economic Conference of 1927, proposals came from many sources

49. *Compte Rendu de la Commission Mixte Franco-Italienne d'Union Douanière, Paris, le 22 janvier 1949* (Paris: Imprimerie Nationale, 1949), p. 96.

50. See Harry D. Gideonse, "Economic Foundations of Pan-Europeanism," *Annals of the American Academy of Political and Social Science*, CXLIX (1930), for the early association of these ideas.

for sponsorship of international cartelization, both as a method of international economic cooperation which would lessen the need for attempts to lower tariff barriers by multilateral agreement and as a method of making tariff reduction safe for high-cost domestic industries. The French were most prominent in furthering these ideas, but they received more or less qualified support from the International Chamber of Commerce and from League of Nations committees and conferences. M. Louis Loucheur, French Minister of Commerce, who was the original sponsor and one of the main participants in the Geneva Economic Conference, was an enthusiastic protagonist of international cartels and of international tariff agreements to facilitate their operation as means of lessening international competition, and the documentation and proceedings of the conference show that his ideas received substantial support. But for the most part the discussion remained on an abstract level.[51]

With the coming of the depression, the search for means of alleviating its impact on Europe through international collaboration led to a revival of the discussion, under League of Nations auspices, of cartels in relation to European "economic union." Various committees and conferences of the League of

---

51. Some of the references to the idea that the multiplication of international cartels would facilitate the reduction of tariffs by reducing the need for them made in the course of the Geneva Economic Conference apparently were related to expositions of the idea which M. Loucheur had made outside the conference. After a series of eulogies of international cartels had been presented in the meetings of the Industry Committee of the conference, a Soviet delegate, Mr. Sokolnikoff, made the following pertinent comment:

"Industrial and commercial ententes would not lead to social and economic peace. The danger of a rise in prices was only too real. This was shown by the fact that it was being proposed to replace Customs Tariffs, the object of which was to maintain prices at a high level, by cartellisation, which enabled the same result to be attained by more modern methods." League of Nations, *Report and Proceedings of the World Economic Conference,* Geneva, 1927 (Document C.356.M.129.1927.II), II, 152.

Nations gave support simultaneously to international cartelization and to multilateral agreements to lower trade barriers,
but there was apparently only one definite proposal to link the
two together as related parts of a single project.

This proposal was made by the French Government to a meeting of the League Commission of Enquiry for European Union
in May, 1931. A strengthening and extension of international
cartel agreements was to be sponsored. Since strong cartels
reserve the national markets for the domestic producers of the
respective acceding countries and limit imports to agreed quotas and prices, tariffs become unnecessary to protect national
industries. The lowering of tariffs, therefore, becomes possible
without adversely affecting the national economies. However,
"the producers in countries which were not disposed to take
part in international agreements would not be allowed to benefit from Customs exemptions." Moreover, the tariff reductions
would amount to a bounty to all who voluntarily accepted the
discipline of the cartel.[52] The French proposed that the League
and the governments take the cartel agreements under their
sponsorship and stimulate the private efforts in this direction.
These agreements would be less difficult to negotiate than a
simultaneous multilateral reduction of tariffs, and would be better than a customs union. Tariffs would be retained, since they
would be needed to forestall dumping, but the duties collected
could be refunded with respect to all products carrying a cartel
certificate.[53]

52. It is not clear to the present writer how a bounty would result for cartel members in non-exporting countries.

53. League of Nations, Commission of Enquiry for European Union, *Minutes of the
Third Session of the Commission,* May 15–21, 1931 (Document C.395. M.158.1931.
VII), pp. 16–24; 79–88.

Nothing came immediately from the French proposal of 1931, but the idea it expounded did not die.[54] In the negotiations for the further development of Benelux, and in the negotiations for the formation of a Franco-Italian customs union, it is clear that much reliance is being placed on cartel agreements, sanctioned and probably also participated in by the member governments, both to eliminate competition in the import and export trade with non-members and to keep within bounds the rivalry for the customs union market between the industries of the respective member countries.[55]

There seems likelihood, therefore, that in the framing of future customs unions and in the development of existing ones, cartel agreements or their equivalent will be used as supplement or substitute for other means of assuring that the removal of the tariff wall between the members of the customs union shall not result in more increase of competition between the industries of the respective member countries than is desired. It is also likely, on the basis of the past record, that a minimum of increase in such competition will be desired. This is a reasonable forecast, I think, despite the fact that the Havana Charter contains the statement (Article 44, paragraph 1) that the members "recognize that the purpose of a customs union or free-trade area should be to facilitate trade between the parties and not to raise barriers to the trade of other Member countries with such parties."

---

54. In a 1937 Report, the Economic Committee of the League of Nations drew attention to the possibility of using cartel agreements as a substitute for prohibitive tariffs in dealing with competition from low-cost producers. "It may be pointed out that this difficulty could be met if arrangements could be reached between the industries concerned which would give an assurance against such excessive competition. Quotas applied solely as guarantees for these arrangements are not open to criticism." League of Nations, Economic Committee, *Remarks on the Present Phase of International Economic Relations,* September, 1937 (Document C.358.M.242.1937. II.B), pp. 14–15.

55. See *supra,* pp. 73–75.

8. The Allocation of Customs Revenues

Whenever customs revenues are important, the method of their allocation as between members of a customs union is almost certain to become a major issue,[56] which has a close counterpart in the controversies which have always arisen in federal unions over the distribution of revenues, or the allocation of taxation rights, as between the central and the regional political authorities. The greater the disparity in economic levels between the members, and the greater the differences as between the members in the customary consumption of imported commodities, the greater is likely to be the difficulty in finding a formula for allocation of customs receipts which will be mutually acceptable.

In the German Zollverein the simplest possible formula of allocation, namely, according to population, was found generally practicable, but modification was necessary in at least two instances for members with relatively high per capita income levels and with specially important trade relations outside the Zollverein; the City of Frankfort was allotted a share in the Zollverein customs receipts approximately four and a half times what it would have been entitled to on a population basis, while the rural districts of Frankfort received a lesser supplement; Hanover also was allowed a supplement. The problem of allocation of revenues as between Germany and Austria arising out of the different economic levels of the two regions was stated by Bismarck in 1864 to constitute an insurmountable obstacle to customs union with Austria:

> I regarded a customs union as an impracticable Utopia on account of the differences in the economic and administrative

---

56. For details as to methods of allocating customs revenues in customs unions, see T. E. Gregory, *Tariffs: A Study in Method* (London, 1921), pp. 16–18, and *Customs Unions*, 1947, pp. 17–19.

conditions of both parties. The commodities which formed the financial basis of the customs union in the north do not come into use at all in the greater part of Austro-Hungarian territory. The difficulties which the differences in habits of life and in consumption between North and South Germany brought about even now within the Zollverein, would be insurmountable, if both districts were to be included in the same customs boundary with the eastern provinces of Austria-Hungary. A fairer scale of distribution, or one more corresponding with the existing consumption of dutiable goods, could not be arrived at; every scale would be either unfair to the Zollverein, or unacceptable to public opinion in Austria-Hungary. There is no common measure of taxation for the Slovack or Galician with his few wants on the one side, and on the other for the inhabitant of the Rhenish provinces and of Lower Saxony.[57]

In the customs unions in which British Crown Colonies participated, as well as in some other customs unions, allocation was in general according to place of consumption. This formula would be difficult to apply either where imported raw materials were processed in one member territory for sale in another, or where wholesale distribution was concentrated in one territory. Two instances can be cited where the application of this formula gave rise either to difficulties of administration or to complaints of inequitable division of revenues.

When the Australian Commonwealth was established, the States were for a five-year period allotted shares in the customs revenue collections of the Commonwealth in proportion to consumption within the States of the imported commodities.

57. *Bismarck the Man and the Statesman: Being the Reflections and Reminiscences of Otto Prince von Bismarck,* translated from the German under the supervision of A. J. Butler (London, 1898), I, 377–78.

Application of this formula involved elaborate bookkeeping, extremely burdensome administrative red tape, and extensive controversy.[58]

In the case of the customs union between Ruanda-Urundi, a territory under League of Nations mandate to Belgium, and the Belgian Congo, duties collected on imports are credited to the territory of destination, which in application is taken to be the territory of last wholesale transaction. A member of the Mandates Commission, Mr. Merlin, in 1926 objected that the wholesale destination was often the Belgian Congo when the ultimate consumption was in Ruanda-Urundi. To this the Belgian representative before the Commission replied "that the situation explained by M. Merlin was the inevitable result of the Customs union the establishment of which was permitted by the mandate, and the consequences of which it was necessary to accept."[59]

In the various South African customs unions where allocation was according to consumption, the territory in which the import duties were actually collected was allowed a fraction of the receipts as compensation for administrative expense. In the Poland-Danzig Customs Union, which was established under League of Nations auspices in accordance with provisions in the Treaty of Peace with Germany following World War I, the allocation of customs revenues was to be by agreement between Poland and Danzig, but with consumption to be taken into account. Agreement was reached that division of total revenues was to be presumptively in accordance with per capita consumption, but that it was to be assumed that average consumption per head in

---

58. See Stephen Mills, *Taxation in Australia* (London, 1925), pp. 200–1.

59. League of Nations, Permanent Mandate Commission, *Minutes of the Ninth Session,* Geneva, 1926, pp. 98–101.

Danzig was six times that in Poland; this arrangement was to be reconsidered at three-year intervals.[60]

In other customs unions receipts were divided according to agreed percentages (e.g., Austria-Modena, 1852; Austria-Liechtenstein, 1852), or a lump sum per annum allocation was made to a small member (e.g., Prussia-Schwarzburg, 1819; Italy-Albania, 1939), or special modifications were made in the allocation-by-consumption or allocation-by-collections formulas. In the Austro-Hungarian Customs Union, as in other cases where customs union was associated with political union, no provision was made for division of customs revenue. In the Austro-Hungarian case, not only did all the customs revenue go into the Dual Kingdom's treasury, but in addition "quotas" were assigned to the constituent states to meet the remainder of the needs of the central government.

An unusual provision was contained in the customs union agreements of 1930 of the Union of South Africa with Northern Rhodesia and with Southern Rhodesia. These agreements were really partial abrogations of the preexisting customs unions. As part of the movement toward tariff autonomy of the Rhodesias, it was provided in these agreements that each of the members of the respective unions was to pay the other specified percentages of the value of its manufactures exported to the other. These provisions seem to be instances where revenues lost as a result of effective protection of the industries of one member in the territory of the other had to be made up by the member profiting by the tariff protection, a type of provision which the Canadian Prairie Provinces, or Western Australia, would no doubt be happy to have applied to their relationships to the Dominion, or the Commonwealth, tariffs.

60. For the Danzig-Poland negotiations, and for general discussion of the problems arising out of the allocation of customs union revenues, see Martin Jos. Funk, *Die danzig-polnische Zollunion: Der bisherige und der künftige Zollverteilungschlüssel* (Jena, 1926).

In the Report of the Second Joint Committee on Franco-Italian Customs Union there is no systematic discussion of the question of the mode of allocation of customs receipts, and the only comment suggests that allocation of receipts by ultimate destination of the imports is planned, and that the technical difficulties associated with this procedure are being seriously underestimated. When a common tariff is in operation—

> the question of transfer of customs receipts will arise only in the case where an importer enters for customs in a territory of the union other than the territory of destination goods which will subsequently be sent on to this latter territory; it would seem that this question can be dealt with in a satisfactory manner, if each of the customs administrations sets up a special statistical service; the two governments could, to this effect, negotiate a special protocol.

Chapter V

Political Aspects of Customs Union

1. The Location of Administrative Authority in Customs Unions

When the tariff wall is removed between two territories with different economic interests and conditions and different loyalties, each territory, if they are of comparable economic importance, acquires a live concern in the character and standards of customs administration within the other territory.[1] If the territories are disproportionate in size, the larger territory has a most urgent interest in the quality of the customs administration in the smaller territory. It therefore is necessary under ordinary circumstances, where there is not complete mutual trust between the members of the customs union, to merge in some degree and fashion the customs-administration staffs of the two (or more) territories.

Six degrees of merger can be distinguished, which, in descending order of completeness of merger, are: (1) complete absorption by the predominant member of the responsibility throughout the territory for enforcement of the customs laws and regulations; (2) a merged central customs and administrative staff, responsible to the customs union as a whole and not to particular members thereof; (3) active participation by officers of

1. Bismarck in 1864 gave as one ground for his opposition to an Austro-German customs union that he "did not believe in the trustworthiness of the service on a great part of the Austrian frontier." *Bismarck the Man and the Statesman, op. cit.,* I, 378.

a predominant member in the administration of the customs of the lesser member or members; (4) supervision by the predominant member of the customs administration of the lesser member or members; (5) mutual supervision; (6) complete autonomy of administration, with reliance upon mutual integrity and efficiency, with provision, perhaps, for resort to arbitration in case of disputes. Corresponding classifications could be made of the allocation of authority with respect to changes in tariffs, or of customs codes, and with respect to the conduct of negotiations with outside countries on tariff matters.

Where customs union occurs between states of greatly disproportionate size, the predominant member usually insists upon complete authority over customs and administration for the entire customs union territory and upon the power of appointment for the entire customs staff. There are important economic reasons why a large member of a customs union should want as complete as possible a monopoly of administrative authority over customs altogether aside from any political or "imperialistic" ambitions it may have. Illustrative of administrative monopoly for the predominant member were the customs unions between Prussia and its enclaves, between France and Monaco, and between Austria and Liechtenstein. The term "customs accession" ("accession douanière," "Zollanschluss") has been applied to customs unions of this type.[2]

The relations of France to Monaco within their customs union provide an extreme illustration of how important control over the administration of customs in a lesser member's territory may be *for economic reasons* to the larger member. When France acquired Savoy, Monaco, except for its bit of coastline on the

2. L. Bosc, *op. cit.*, p. 69, has collected the following German terms, all used, with or without attempts at distinction, to designate customs union: Zollverein, Zollvereinigung, Zolleinigung, Zollanschluss, Zollverband, Zollbündniss, Zollgemeinschaft, Zoll-liga, Zoll-koalition, Wirtschaftliche Allianz, Wirtschaftverein.

Mediterranean, became a French enclave. The French interest in customs union with Monaco, which at the time had a population of under 1500, was primarily to acquire the authority and means to prevent the smuggling into France via Monaco of commodities subject in France to high import duties or excise taxes. Since all collections of import duties went to the customs union as a whole for subsequent allocation irrespective of where they had been collected, and since the Monaco share in the total customs revenues was too small to give it a substantial interest in their full collection, laxity of collection in Monaco would bring it but a trifling loss in customs revenue, whereas properly designed laxity could bring it considerable profit in other directions. Monacan officials could collect bribes for evasion of customs; reputation for laxity could bring increased business to the port of Monaco as a port of entry for goods destined for France; smuggling into France could provide a remunerative occupation for residents of Monaco; it could become a specially attractive location for plants processing dutiable imported raw materials for the French market. Complete or nearly complete French administration of customs in Monaco was the only effective way in which France could assure herself against circumvention of the French tariff and excise régimes.[3]

The German Zollverein in the course of its evolution provided for almost every possible form of allocation of administrative authority over customs as between the members. While what James Russell Lowell once said of German federal union—that

---

3. A detailed account of the history and mode of operation of the France-Monaco Customs Union is given in Gabriel Farnet, *Les relations douanières entre la France et la Principauté de Monaco* (1917). The author, writing from the point of view of Nice, a rival port and commercial center, may not be altogether fair to Monaco, but he argued that even "accession douanière" had not sufficed to prevent Monacan ingenuity from finding loopholes in the French tariff wall, and he urged the need of still further limitations on Monacan autonomy.

it "could not fail to resemble the compact between a lion, half a dozen foxes, and a score of mice"—had some applicability also to the German Zollverein, circumstances forced Prussia at first to act with great circumspection in this respect, and even with great generosity. The coercive power which her transit duties gave her over the enclave states enabled her to induce them to accept full Prussian customs domination. The other German states, however, had to be wooed, or wooed and coerced, if they were to be induced to enter the Zollverein and to remain in it once entered, and their fear of Prussian political expansionism made them especially jealous of their sovereignty with respect to legislative and administrative authority. For some time also, some of them were able to offset in part their weakness in dealing with Prussia when operating alone by forming smaller customs unions of their own. The southern German states, moreover, could pit Austria against Prussia, if Prussian economic or political pressure on them were made too irksome.[4] Until the defeat of Austria in the War of 1866, therefore, Prussia was obliged to share authority in the Zollverein on a substantially equal basis with at least most of the other non-enclave members, so that on major questions of tariff revision and administration Prussia with its 17,000,000 population and, for example, Brunswick, with 200,000 population, had, at least contractually, equal authority.[5]

4. Another form of defense of the lesser German states against coercion applied individually to them to enter the Prussian Zollverein was the defensive league of eighteen states negotiated at Cassel in 1828; no member of the league was to participate in a customs union without consent of all the members. The league collapsed in 1831, when Electoral Hesse, a member, accepted membership in the Prussian Zollverein.

5. The status of Luxemburg in the Zollverein under the 1839 agreement with Prussia was made subordinate, however, to that of Prussia. Prussia refused Luxemburg an autonomous role in the Zollverein, on the ground that Luxemburg was bound dynastically with the Netherlands, which could have conflicting interests with the

The smaller the state, however, the less secure it was likely to feel if officials of a powerful neighbor could operate on its territory, and the more jealous also it would be that there should be no impairment of the trappings of its sovereignty. It is, therefore, mostly in the treaties of customs union between great states and very small ones that there are elaborate provisions with respect to the relative authority of officials, the uniforms to be worn, and so forth. The necessity of ceding to the sensitivity of small countries also often meant that in practice the potential administrative economies of customs union were not realized, or were only very partially realized. The fear of political unification acted as a barrier to full exploitation of the administrative benefits of tariff unification.

2. Customs Union and Neutrality Obligations

In the Austria-Modena case, as we have seen, international complications arose from the fact that the customs arrangement did not go far enough. There have been at least two occasions when proposed customs unions aroused major international controversy because they went too far—the proposal for Franco-Belgian customs union in the 1840's and the Austro-German Anschluss project of 1931, both of which foundered. In each case the external opposition centered on treaty obligations to maintenance of the independence of the lesser member of the projected customs

Zollverein. Luxemburg was therefore represented in Zollverein deliberations only through Prussian mediation, customs administration in Luxemburg was placed in charge of the Cologne office of the Prussian customs authorities, and at least half of the customs guards in Luxemburg were required to be Prussian officials.

Other German states also accepted subordinate status to Prussia in some respects; e.g., the adoption of excise regimes uniform with that of Prussia, and the adoption of the Prussian customs code.

union and on the alleged threat to its independence which customs union with a larger and stronger neighbor would involve.

(a) The Franco-Belgian Customs Union Project of the 1840's

Belgium, upon its revolt from Holland in 1830, was set up as an independent country with a guarantee by the great European powers of its neutrality. Discussion of customs union with France began almost at once, but came to nothing. In 1840, however, on Belgian initiative, more serious negotiations were embarked upon, culminating in four conferences in Paris presided over by M. Guizot, the French prime minister. These negotiations also petered out, because of both difficulties in reaching agreement and strong opposition by England and Prussia. It is the latter only which is of special interest at this point.

In the negotiations between the Belgians and the French, the French objectives were primarily political and the Belgian ones economic. The Belgians were prepared to accept the total abolition of a tariff wall between the two countries and the establishment of a common tariff at the other frontiers. The French insisted, however, upon complete French executive control (*pouvoir executif*) of the customs administration and on the right to place French customs officials on Belgian soil. This the Belgians strongly resisted: the admission of several thousand French customs officers in uniform on Belgian territory would constitute "a fatal threat to the independence and the neutrality of Belgium." The negotiations continued, and in November, 1842, a draft of a treaty was discussed which provided for the adoption by Belgium of the principal features of the French customs regime. But there was internal opposition on economic grounds in both countries, as well as external pressure hostile to the proposed customs union, and the negotiations were allowed quietly to lapse.

Guizot later questioned whether Belgium really wanted customs union, and claimed that he did not regret the failure to reach agreement. He had become convinced that the economic disadvantages outweighed the political advantages for France. "We would have found in this arrangement a satisfaction of vanity rather than a solid accession of strength and power." Belgium would have retained its spirit of independence and nationality and the relations between the two countries would have encountered many disturbances. The great powers would have protested, and in any case would have felt profoundly injured and disquieted as to French policy and would have formed anti-French coalitions. The principal French industries would have been injured and internal dissension in France would have resulted.[6]

The protests from abroad, formal on the part of Great Britain, informal on the part of Prussia, turned on the issue whether a Belgo-French customs union would constitute a violation of the international guarantee, by treaties of 1831 and 1839, of the neutrality of Belgium. Palmerston took the position that every union between two countries in commercial matters must necessarily tend to a community of action in the political field also, but that, when such community is established between a great power and a small one, the will of the stronger must prevail, and the real and practical independence of the smaller country will be lost. He attached great significance to the proposed establishment of French customs officials on Belgian soil as of itself constituting a major surrender of Belgian administrative independence, from which the loss of political independence would be only a step.

Guizot replied that the project would involve only a "special form of commercial treaty" and, far from threatening the

---

6. F. P. J. Guizot, *Mémoires pour servir à l'histoire de mon temps* (Paris-Leipzig, 1858–1867), VI, 276–96; A. Dechamps, "Une page d'histoire," *Revue générale*, 1869, I, 554–55; see also F. De Launoy, "Les projets d'union douanière franco-belge en 1841–42," *Revue catholique des idées et des faits* (Brussels), December, 1922.

independence of either country, would be on the part of Belgium "an act and proof of independence," especially since Belgium would retain the right to end the customs union if it found it threatening to its independence. It would be a "bizarre independence" which Belgium would enjoy if such contractual relations as were in her interest and perhaps even were essential to her continued existence were prohibited.[7]

(b) The Austro-German Anschluss, 1931

The major issues raised by the proposed Austro-German Anschluss in 1931 were fundamentally the same as those to which the Franco-Belgian customs union project of the 1840's had given rise, and the outcome was also the same—the abandonment of the project under external pressure.

The Franco-Belgian precedent was not much referred to in the Anschluss controversy, but this need occasion no surprise. Aside from the fact that the relevant historical material was only superficially exploited in the briefs presented by the participants, the Franco-Belgian precedent was an embarrassing one for several of the participants in the international debate over the Anschluss. France had denied in the Franco-Belgian case what she was insisting upon now, that customs union between a small and weak country and a neighboring large and powerful one was a threat to the political independence of the small country. There was a similar, though opposite, reversal of the

7. Guizot, *op. cit.*; Alfred de Ridder, *Les projets d'union douanière franco-belge et les puissances européennes, 1836–1843* (Brussels, 1933), pp. 34–41. De Ridder, who made use of unpublished British and Austrian foreign office archives, reports that Metternich, on behalf of Austria, substantially accepted Guizot's claim that customs union would not constitute a violation of neutrality obligations. He refused to draw a sharp distinction between customs union and other forms of commercial arrangements, and found it puzzling how Prussia in particular could subscribe to the Palmerston thesis that customs union was "political suicide" for smaller countries.

roles of Prussia in the 1840's and Germany in 1931. Austria's attitude in the two cases was consistent enough,[8] but the collapse of the Franco-Belgian project under the hostile pressure of the great powers made it inexpedient to cite it as a precedent in its own favor.

Post-World-War-I Austria was bound by two international treaties not to alienate her independence: Article 88 of the Treaty of Peace, Saint-Germain, September 10, 1919, and Protocol No. 1 of October 4, 1922, of the Agreement for Financial Assistance to Austria. Their texts were as follows:

ARTICLE 88. The independence of Austria is inalienable otherwise than with the consent of the Council of the League of Nations. Consequently Austria undertakes in the absence of the consent of the said Council to abstain from any act which might directly or indirectly or by any means whatever compromise her independence, particularly, and until her

---

8. One phase of the 1917–1918 negotiations of Austria and Germany for closer post-war economic relations between the two countries would have been embarrassing, however, for Austria as well as for Germany if it had been brought into the record. The German negotiators then held that whatever arrangements were reached must preserve the full sovereignty of each of the participating states. Any arrangement reached for closer economic relations must therefore avoid being juristically "municipal" (*staatsrechtlicher*) in nature, and must remain wholly within the limits of an "international" (*völkerrechtlicher*) agreement. There could consequently be no question of a full customs union, since this would involve the establishment of special institutions of a municipal character (*staatsrechtlicher Gemeinschaftsorgane*). The Austrian negotiators wanted to go further beyond an ordinary commercial treaty than the German proposals, but they agreed that "the arrangement should be made to rest on an 'international' (*völkerrechtlicher*) foundation and could not be given the character of a customs union." Gustav Gratz and Richard Schüller, *Die äussere Wirtschaftspolitik Österreich-Ungarns, Mitteleuropäische Pläne* (Vienna, 1925), pp. 67–69. The treatment of this episode in the version in English of this book (Gratz and Schüller, *The Economic Policy of Austria-Hungary during the War in Its External Relations* [New Haven, 1928], p. 45) is so compressed as to be misleading. See *infra*, pp. 105 ff., for an account of the final outcome of these negotiations.

admission to membership of the League of Nations, by participation in the affairs of another Power.[9]

Protocol No. 1. [Austria] undertakes, in accordance with the terms of Article 88 of the Treaty of St. Germain, not to alienate its independence; it will abstain from any negotiations or from any economic or financial engagement calculated directly or indirectly to compromise this independence.

This undertaking shall not prevent Austria from maintaining, subject to the provisions of the Treaty of St. Germain, her freedom in the matter of customs tariffs and commercial or financial agreements, and, in general, in all matters relating to her economic regime or her commercial relations, provided always that she shall not violate her economic independence by granting to any State a special regime or exclusive advantages calculated to threaten this independence.[10]

Austria had to face the prospect of attack on the legality of the proposed arrangement with Germany from two different directions—that the arrangement was in violation of Austria's most-favored-nation obligations and that the arrangement involved an alienation or threat of alienation of Austrian sovereignty. The further the arrangement went or appeared to go in the direction of economic unification with Germany, the greater its vulnerability to legal attack on the latter score but the smaller its vulnerability on the former score. It seems clear that the language of the Anschluss agreement was carefully chosen to steer between these two perils and it is probable also that the particular form and substance given to the administrative

---

9. *The Treaties of Peace, 1919–1923* (New York: Carnegie Endowment for International Peace, 1924), Vol. I, p. 297.

10. League of Nations, *Treaty Series*, Vol. 12, pp. 387–89; M. O. Hudson, *International Legislation* (Washington, 1931–), II, 882–84.

arrangements can be explained in part at least by the necessity of facing simultaneously these threats from opposite directions. Thus the term "customs union" is never used in the text of the Anschluss agreement, presumably to make it, in appearance at least, less different from an ordinary commercial treaty, while the standard conditions of a customs union—common tariff, abolition of an internal tariff wall between the partners, provision for allocation of customs revenues—were all included, although so formulated as to minimize as much as possible the impression of economic and administrative fusion of the two countries in tariff matters.

When the legality of the project was questioned before the League of Nations, the issue was by general consent referred to the Permanent Court of International Justice for an advisory opinion. Manifestation of the strength of the opposition to the Anschluss in France, Italy, and the succession countries of the Austro-Hungarian Empire, perhaps also French promises of financial aid to Austria if the project were dropped and the anticipation of an unfavorable decision by the Court, led Austria and Germany to announce their abandonment of the project a few days before the Court issued its opinion.

The Court found that the Anschluss would be in violation of Austria's legal obligations. The Court divided badly, the majority opinion carrying by only one vote over the dissenters, and every judge voting in conformity with the political alignment or the political sympathies of the country of which he was a national, where this country had a special interest. Public opinion in England and in the United States, as in neutral European countries, was very nearly unanimous in regretting and even in condemning the decision, as having been over-influenced by "political" considerations which the Court was serving by means of a narrow legalism. Even in France, the decision was frankly approved on purely political grounds, and its political necessity somewhat apologetically defended. General sympathy with Austria's desperate economic plight, for which customs union with Germany seemed to offer at least a partial remedy; the general belief that customs union is a "liberal" device, a movement in the direction of free trade; the fact that some of the countries opposing the Anschluss were themselves promoting schemes for customs unions, "European Union," and so forth, and attributing to the multitude of national tariff walls in Europe part responsibility for Europe's economic ills; impatience with France's intransigence toward the defeated Central Powers; the alignment of the Court's members along the lines of their political affiliations—all of these combined to give the Court's findings a very bad press indeed, and to give a serious blow to the prestige of the Court.

With the aid of the hindsight which later developments have made possible, it is not as clear now as it then seemed that the Court's decision was either legally or politically a mistake. The Court made its finding rest mainly on the ground that customs union with Germany would be in violation of Austria's obligation under the 1922 Protocol not to "violate her economic independence by granting to any State a special regime or exclusive advantages calculated to threaten this independence." A measure which would closely entangle the Austrian with the German economy and from which after some years of operation Austria could withdraw only at the cost of great economic shock was, given the relative strength of the two countries and the past history of Germany, to say nothing of her later history, one which could be reasonably held to be "calculated to threaten" Austrian independence. As customs unions go, the Anschluss agreement contemplated one closer than most. It is a justifiable inference that the drafters of the Protocol of 1922 intended to forestall just this type of arrangement, for otherwise it is hard to conceive what they could have had in mind.[11]

3. Customs Union and Political Unification

Many movements for customs union have had no solid foundation in the basic and powerful economic and political forces in the communities concerned, and have therefore evaporated before reaching even the stage of serious negotiation. Of the more serious movements which involved a great power and a small country or a number of small countries, it appears to have been the case without exception for the great power that political objectives were the important ones, while the economic consequences of customs union were regarded without enthusiasm or even accepted only as a necessary price which had to be paid to promote a political end. For small countries considering customs union with great powers, on the other hand, only the economic consequences as a rule were regarded as attractive, while the political aspects were thought of as involving risks which might have to be accepted for the sake of the economic benefits with which they were unfortunately associated.

Only where the prospective partners have not been greatly disparate in size, or where neither has been a great power (so that the contingency that at some stage in the relations between them within the customs union the stronger partner would resort to force or to economic coercions to impose political union or hegemony on the other has not arisen), has the question of

11. On the Anschluss controversy, see League of Nations, *Official Journal* for 1931, *passim*; Permanent Court of International Justice, *Customs Régime between Germany and Austria*, Series C, No. 53; M. Margaret Ball, *Post-War German-Austrian Relations; The Anschluss Movement, 1918–1936* (1937).

customs union been dealt with as wholly or predominantly an economic question, unembellished or untainted by political hopes or political fears. Where serious political aspirations have come into the picture in such cases, and all the prospective members were small countries, the aspirations have usually taken the form of hopes that economic union between the weak would ripen into political union, and that by the political union of the weak a power might be established strong enough to defend against aggression from outside. At least since the days when territorial windfalls through dynastic succession became impossible or highly improbable, coercion or fear of coercion has been an essential element in the union of independent states into larger political wholes. States have been absorbed through coercion by larger states; states have united voluntarily in order to forestall coercion by other states; ethnic groups have broken away from alien rule by force or threat of force, their own or that of external friends, to join with their fellows. With rare exceptions, the process of state formation has been a process of coercion or of the pursuit of security against coercion.

Whatever role economic factors have played in the process of state formation has therefore been a secondary one. The nature of this role, and especially the part which unification of tariffs has played and can play in it, has not as yet been subjected to systematic study, either in the abstract or by appeal to historical experience. It has consequently been easy for writers to fall into sweeping generalizations in this field. One of these generalizations is that economic unification must precede political unification, or, less extreme, that economic unification tends powerfully to lead to political unification. The idea that commerce promotes friendly relations between peoples is, of course, an ancient one. But even the doctrine that economic union, by promoting friendship, would promote political unification received formulation at least as early as the seventeenth century.

In 1665, Bishop Roxas, a Hungarian acting on behalf of the Austrian emperor, launched a project for a union directed against France between Austria, Spain, and Bavaria, the political alliance to be fostered through a preceding economic union. The economic union was to begin with Austria and Bavaria, with other German princes to be drawn in later through separate negotiations. The union was to have a common tariff, with lower duties for other German countries regarded as potential members. Spain also was to receive preferential treatment; the union should seek eventually to bring Spain in as a full member, because of its importance as an export market and as a source of West Indian gold and silver. For Roxas, and for Johann Joachim Becher, a distinguished Austrian mercantilist whose services he enlisted in promoting his projects, its merit lay in its proposal to use economic collaboration as a means of fostering willingness to accept alliance. As Becher wrote:

> The union of hearts comes into being immediately upon one person helping another to prosperity, and becomes strengthened if the aim is to establish a perpetual increase and community of riches. Nothing is stronger than this bond, since no cunning and not even a bloody sword can dissolve it.[12]

In the great tariff debate which took place in England in 1903, one of the major arguments for the abandonment of free trade was that it would make possible the establishment

---

12. See Michael Döberl, "Das Projekt einer Einigung Deutschlands auf wirtschaftlicher Grundlage a.d.J. 1665," *Forschungen sur Geschichte Bayerns*, VI (1898), 163–205.

The project was not regarded as practicable even within Austria, and Bavaria was definitely hostile to it. Bavaria was not interested in political alliance with Austria, but was interested in getting financial aid. Such aid was not available from Austria, which was itself seeking loans in Holland, but was available from France in the form of subsidies, at the price of a political alliance against Austria. Bavaria shortly after did enter into an alliance with France.

of a system of British Empire tariff preferences, often referred to as a "Zollverein," and that the closer commercial ties which would result would facilitate a closer political unification of the Empire. Joseph Chamberlain claimed in the course of the debate that "in all previous cases commercial union preceded political union" and Arthur Balfour cited the relations between England and Scotland as an instance where "fiscal union has been the prelude to that closer and more intimate union which is the basis of national strength," while the German Zollverein was freely appealed to as a precedent very much in point. On the free-trade side, W. R. Scott, and others, replied to Balfour's citation of Scotland in support of the thesis that political union was normally preceded by commercial union, that in fact the political union of England and Scotland was preceded by tariff war and trade war; it was the desire to end this, on the Scottish side for economic reasons and on the English side for political and strategic reasons—England was then engaged in war with France, and there was some danger that Scotland would give aid to France—which was the major factor in bringing about the political union of 1707.[13]

Gustav Schmoller was later to write that the German Zollverein was "the one considerable exception to the historical law that political union tends to precede commercial union."[14] Schmoller could have derived his "historical law" from Friedrich List, the apostle of economic nationalism. Writing in or before 1841, List could affirm the universal applicability of

13. See W. R. Scott, "The Fiscal Policy of Scotland before the Union," *Scottish Historical Review*, I (1904), 173–90. Cf. also Theodora Keith, "Commercial Relations of England and Scotland, 1663–1707," *Girton College Studies* No. 1 (Cambridge, England, 1910); *idem*, "The Economic Causes for the Scottish Union," *English Historical Review*, XXIV (1909), 44–60.

14. "Die Handels- und Zollannäherung Mitteleuropas," *Jahrbuch für Gesetzgebung, Verwaltung, und Volkswirtschaft*, XL (1916), 529.

the law without making an exception for Germany. According to List:

> A true principle...underlies the system of the popular [cosmopolitan, free-trade] school, but a principle which must be recognized and applied by science if its design to enlighten practice is to be fulfilled, an idea which practice cannot ignore without getting astray; only the school has omitted to take into consideration the nature of nationalities and their special interests and conditions, and to bring these into accord with the idea of universal union and everlasting peace.
>
> The popular school has assumed as being actually in existence a state of things which has yet to come into existence. It assumes the existence of a universal union and a state of perpetual peace, and deduces therefrom the great benefits of free trade. In this manner it confounds effects with causes. Among the provinces and states which are already politically united, there exists a state of perpetual peace; from this political union originates their commercial union, and it is in consequence of the perpetual peace thus maintained that the commercial union has become so beneficial to them. All examples which history can show are those in which the political union has led the way, and the commercial has followed. Not a single instance can be adduced in which the latter has taken the lead, and the former has grown up from it.[15]

The historical record does seem to support List's and Schmoller's proposition, at least if it is not made a question of "historical law" and if it is presented merely as a generalization

---

15. Friedrich List, *The National System of Political Economy* [1841], Sampson S. Lloyd, *tr.* (New York, 1904), pp. 102–3.

as to past political unions that they preceded (or were simultaneous with) commercial union.

We tend today to take the identity of political and economic frontiers for granted, but it is in fact a quite modern phenomenon, and by no means a universal one even now. With respect to tariffs, which are our special concern here, it was almost a general rule until comparatively recently that the area of political unification was greater than the area of tariff unification. In the Middle Ages customs collectors were frequently stationed, not at the boundaries, but in the interior of political units, at important market centers, at junctions of trade routes, or at Alpine passes. Originally, customs duties were levied for purely fiscal purposes, and it was only as they began to be used as instruments of "national" commercial (and political) policy that there was any marked tendency to unify them nationally and to confine them to political frontiers. Regional separatism and local vested interests retarded the process, and it was not until late in the eighteenth century that any considerable country had a single tariff applied only at its political frontiers. Colbert's famous tariff of 1664 was the first major step in this direction in any country, but it unified only the customs of "les douze provinces" and "les cinq grosses fermes"; "les provinces à l'instar de l'étranger effectif" were left completely, and "les provinces réputées étrangères" were left partially, outside the central tariff area. It was not until the French Revolution, in 1790, that the French tariff was completely unified. The customs tariff of Austria was not unified until 1775, and even then only with respect to Austria proper; tariff walls continued as between Austria, Hungary, the Tyrol, Transylvania, and Lombardy-Venice, until the 1850's and later. There were in Prussian territory until 1818 over sixty sets of customs duties, and this was only partially to be explained by the discontinuous character of the Prussian territories and the existence within these territories of enclaves with independent sovereignty. The customs unification of Great Britain and Ireland began only with their parliamentary union in 1801, and was not completed until 1826. The Channel Islands are still outside the British tariff wall. The Spanish tariff line was not moved north to the Pyrenees until after 1840. It was not until the middle of last century that Denmark had a single uniform tariff throughout its territories, and Czarist Russia never had one. Switzerland did not have a unified tariff system until 1848. Under the Articles of Confederation, each of the states in the American Union had its separate tariff, and a common tariff for all the United States came only with the Federal Constitution of 1787.

Aside from the German Zollverein case, there appear to have been only three instances where substantial tariff unification preceded political union, and in none of these cases can it be held that the tariff unification was in any way responsible for creating a sentiment favorable to political union, or that it in any other significant way made a substantial contribution to the eventual realization of political unity.

The principalities of Moldavia and Wallachia, while still under Turkish suzerainty, wanted political union as well as independence from Turkey. In 1847 the two Principalities signed a convention which abolished customs duties between the two countries, the maximum step toward union which they could at the time venture to take. Political union was approached by gradual steps and was finally achieved in 1878.[16]

"Reciprocity" between Hawaii and the United States preceded by many years the annexation of Hawaii by the United States. In Hawaii a ruling class of American origin had no sentimental interest in Hawaiian independence but had a very strong economic interest in the maintenance of a preferred status for

16. Cf. W. G. East, *The Union of Moldavia and Wallachia, 1859* (Cambridge, England, 1929).

Hawaiian sugar in the highly protected American market. They were quite ready, therefore, and even anxious, to trade Hawaiian independence for tariff-free entrance of Hawaiian sugar into the American market. On the American side, strategic considerations, plus the general expansionist sentiment which was then running strong, led to willingness to assume political responsibility for an economic liability.

In South Africa, a South African Customs Union preceded the establishment of the Union of South Africa. Economic considerations were important in bringing about the political union, but membership in the earlier Customs Union was for the former Boer Republics an act of submission to external authority rather than voluntary. The strength of the political Union, however, such as it was, did derive mainly from its economic implications. There was little unity of national sentiment between the predominantly English and the predominantly Boer colonies, even in their attitudes towards the black—and "colored"—natives who constituted the great mass of the population; and membership in the British Empire was never an enthusiasm of the Afrikanders and is now apparently regarded by a large majority of them as a relationship to be terminated as soon as appears practicable.

The German Zollverein was the pioneer and by far the most important customs union, and generalizations about the origin, nature, and consequences of unification of tariffs tend to be based mainly or wholly on the German experience. Here, indeed, political unification did follow customs union, and it seems to be the general conclusion of historians that customs union did serve both to foster throughout at least the larger part of the territory within the customs union a national sentiment toward political union of the German people and to facilitate the technical and diplomatic task of negotiating political union when the time had become ripe for it. Even in the case of Germany, however, the path from economic to political unification was not a straight and easy one.

The first stage in the evolution of the German Zollverein was the negotiation by Prussia of customs union with the enclave states within the Prussian frontiers, beginning with Schwarzburg-Sondershausen in 1819 and continuing until, with the arrangement with Waldeck in 1831, all the Prussian enclaves had been incorporated in the Prussian tariff system. These small enclaves were predominantly free-trade or low-tariff territories. Partly in order to make customs union more attractive to them, Prussia had in 1818 adopted a new tariff lower than that of any other important country at the time. To add coercion to bribe, Prussia at the same time adopted a new system of heavy transit duties, which bore heavily on the trade of the enclaves with each other and with the outside world. As these transit duties were specific duties and world prices fell markedly after 1818 until the late 1840's, their burden on enclaves and on neighboring states which stayed outside the Prussian customs union became increasingly heavy. There was no way of escape from them except through acceptance of customs union with Prussia on Prussian terms, which meant, as far as the enclaves were concerned, no share in the framing of the Prussian tariff or in its administration.

The customs union agreement of 1828 between Prussia and Hesse-Darmstadt was the first instance of a state accepting the Prussian tariff regime on a substantially voluntary basis and on terms of equality in tariff legislation and administration. This agreement provided the model for subsequent Prussian agreements with non-enclave states. By these agreements, changes in the tariff could be made only by mutual consent and customs administration remained in charge of the different states, subject only to an agreed common administrative code and to allocation of customs revenues among the participating states (generally according to population). By 1867, the German Zollverein included all the German territory later to comprise Imperial Germany, except the Free Cities of Hamburg and Bremen, and these remained outside the German customs system even for some time after 1871.

It is generally agreed that Prussia engineered the customs union primarily for political reasons, in order to gain hegemony or at least influence over the lesser German states.[17] It was largely in order to make certain that the hegemony should be Prussian and not Austrian that Prussia continually opposed Austrian entry into the Union, either openly or by pressing for a customs union tariff lower than highly protectionist Austria could stomach.

The rivalry between Prussia and Austria for the friendship of the lesser German states made it necessary for Prussia to accept a position within the Zollverein which in form at least made her only the leader among equals instead of the predominant partner, and this she found galling. Bismarck, in a memorandum to the King of Prussia, December 25, 1862, proposed the negotiation with France by Prussia of an additional article to the Franco-Zollverein

---

17. Cf. the Report of the Prussian Finance Minister von Motz to Frederick William of Prussia, June, 1827, cited in H. von Treitschke, "Aus den Papieren des Staats-ministers von Motz," *Preussische Jahrbücher,* XXXIX (1877), 412–14:

"[A tariff and commercial union with the lesser German states] offers first, *commercial* advantages.... In addition, there are, secondly, *financial* advantages.... Thirdly, and more important, is the *political* advantage. If it is a truism of political science that tariffs are merely the consequence of the political separation of different states, so must it be true also that the union of these states in a tariff and commercial alliance will bring in its train their union in one and the same political system.... Fourth, this trade system would bring us a military reinforcement of 92,000 men....

"In this alliance, which is founded on a natural basis and upon mutual interests, and which is expanding where it is indispensable, in the middle of Germany, there will arise a new Germany, truly united, strong internally and externally, and under the protection of Prussia. I only hope that what is still lacking will be supplied and that what we have accomplished already will be perfected and maintained with even more caution and circumspection."

Commercial Treaty (which had been signed earlier that year, but had not yet been ratified by the other members of the Zollverein), by which France would undertake, as long as the treaty remained in force between France and Prussia, not to negotiate directly with any other member of the Zollverein, and after February 1, 1866, when the Zollverein Agreement would be up for renewal, not to grant conventional tariff treatment to countries now members of the Zollverein unless they accepted the terms proposed by Prussia.

In support of his argument that Prussia needed to acquire a greater preponderance of power in the Zollverein, Bismarck cited a long list of complaints as to its present working. With Zollverein policy decided by standard diplomatic procedures, all the major members had equal status and unanimity was required to institute tariff or administrative changes and to negotiate effectively with non-member states. It might therefore be the happiest result for Prussia if it could obtain release from the whole network of Bund agreements. As it was, the Zollverein and Bund were in combination a hindrance rather than an aid to the exercise of the full weight of Prussian power with respect both to the great powers and to Prussia's weak neighbors. Were it not for the Bund, Prussia's relations with her weak neighbors would in their natural course develop in the same pattern as Austria's former relations with the small Italian states.[18] Writing in 1864 to Von Rechberg, the Prussian foreign minister, he remarked that "I do not doubt that it would have a happy outcome, if we kept in mind the good adage 'que mal étreint qui trop embrasse,' if we ceased to accept delay in obtaining the benefits of a commercial treaty [with France] because of our pursuit of the will-of-the wisp of customs unification."[19]

18. Bismarck, *Die gesammelten Werke* (Berlin, 2d ed.), IV (1927), 30–34.

19. *Ibid.*, p. 553. Bismarck had expressed similar views earlier, in 1857 and 1858. See *Correspondance diplomatique de M. de Bismarck (1851–1859)*, translated from the original German edition of H. von Poschinger (Paris, 1883), II, 307 ff.; II, 423 ff.

The defeat of Austria by Prussia in the Seven-Weeks War of 1866 resulted in a drastic change of status of Prussia in the Zollverein. The alignment in this war showed little evidence that the Zollverein had fostered political unity. Most of the members of the Zollverein fought with Austria against Prussia, whereas Oldenburg and the three free cities of Hamburg, Bremen, and Luebeck, which were not members of the Zollverein, were allies of Prussia in the war. As part of the fruits of victory, Prussia annexed Hanover, Hesse-Cassel, Nassau, Schleswig-Holstein, and Frankfort, which had been aligned against her; and the enlarged and victorious Prussia obtained a reconstitution of the Zollverein on a new basis, under which there was substituted for the diplomatic Customs Conferences of previous years, in which most of the states participated, in form at least, as sovereign units, a Customs Council which reached decisions binding on all by majority vote, and in which Prussia was given a vote of 17 out of a total number of votes of 58. There was also set up a Customs Parliament, with simple majority voting, but with limited powers. Customs inspectors, instead of being local civil servants, were now Zollverein officers. Prussia summoned and dissolved the Customs Council, and her representative presided over its deliberations. Prussia could veto a decision altering existing customs regulations. Prussia summoned, prorogued, and dissolved the Customs Parliament. Prussia signed commercial treaties with other countries on behalf of the Zollverein as a whole.[20] A solid foundation had been laid for the future German Reich, but the evidence would indicate that Prussian might, rather than a common zeal for political unification arising out of an economic partnership, had played the major role.

20. W. O. Henderson, *The Zollverein, op. cit.*, is the principal source for the material presented here relating to the German Zollverein.

The defeat of France by Prussia in 1870 was accompanied by a wave of German national enthusiasm which enabled Prussia to brush aside all remaining opposition to a unified German state under Prussian domination and with the Prussian dynasty at its head.

Whatever may be the lesson to be drawn from the history of the German Zollverein, there are other instances where customs unification was associated with political union, without making the political union impregnable and perhaps even without adding to its strength. In the case of Austria-Hungary, whatever was the strength of the political tie, it was for Hungary weakened by the association with it of the customs union with Austria, and the continuance of the customs union was in constant jeopardy until the break-up of the Austro-Hungarian Empire in 1918. There was an approach to customs union during the period of political union between Norway and Sweden, but it did not suffice to prevent an effective separatist movement in Norway. In several federal unions, the common tariff operates as an irritant and as a mild stimulant to separatist movements for some members of the union, instead of as a politically unifying factor. Such is the case with Western Australia in the Australian Commonwealth, and the Prairie Provinces in Canada, and such was the case with the Southern States in the American Union when the Federal tariff became seriously protectionist. In such situations political union tends to be welcomed for the sake of the tariff unity by the regions which believe they profit from the tariff unity, but whatever feeling there is for political unity in the other sections on sentimental or strategic or other economic grounds tends to be undermined by the association of the political union with the tariff union. Relaxation of the tariff unity may then serve to strengthen the political union, or even be an essential requirement if the union is not to dissolve. Such seems to have been the manner of its operation in Austria-Hungary. The

German Zollverein was a more complete customs union despite the separate sovereignties than was Austria-Hungary with its common dynasty. Nevertheless, the Austro-Hungarian customs union, incomplete as it was, involved more economic union than Hungary would accept, and before World War I everything was slated for a substantial dissolution of the customs union when its next revision had come due. It then looked as if refusal of Austria to consent to the sundering of the close economic ties would result in Hungary moving to break all ties. In the case of Ireland, tariff unification was clearly inadequate to weaken a traditional desire for political independence, and close economic ties between Ireland and Great Britain have survived the political separation of these countries.

Large states tend to favor, small states to be suspicious of or violently hostile to, political integration with their neighbors, but even large states are sometimes more reluctant to accept political union because tariff unification is associated with it than they would be, say, in a world in which there was universal free trade so that tariff relations were not a factor to be taken into consideration one way or the other.[21] On the other hand, where the pull of national sentiment in a counter direction is strong, it is remarkable how little avail the most powerful economic incentives can have. The people of the Saar, of Danzig, of Trieste, forced to choose as between nationality and the promise of economic prosperity, voted decisively for nationality. Where

---

21. As long as the United Provinces were able to close the mouth of the Scheldt to commerce with Antwerp, they had no zeal for the independence of the Belgian Netherlands from Spain or even, later, for their union with Holland. Political union would make Dutch restrictions on Belgian commerce appear "fratricidal" if the Dutch and the Belgians were joined in a single political community. Cf. S. T. Bindoff, *The Scheldt Question to 1839* (London, 1945), pp. 116–17. No one, I presume, would deny that the fact that independence of the Philippines would make it easier to abolish free entry of Philippine products into the American market had something to do with the readiness with which the United States granted independence.

the issue has been sharply drawn, the writer knows of no case where the decision has gone in the opposite direction.

Since the rise of nationalism, the voluntary political fusion of hitherto independent states has never come easily, and has never come at all unless it was preceded by close associations of language, culture, and "race," or was aided by the obvious need for unity in defense against an external danger. The economic unity associated with political union may in the net have been more of a hindrance than an aid to the formation of such unions. In any case, the common belief that economic unions bring as a natural product political union has little historical evidence to support it. The saying that "a Zollverein is not a fatherland" attributed to Renan would not be much less true if it were amended to "a Zollverein does not become a fatherland." It is a serious mistake, although a widely prevalent one, to transfer from the field of free trade in general, where it is probably true, to the field of preferential tariff relations between pairs or small groups of countries, where there is no reason at all to believe that it is true, the ancient proposition that the removal of barriers to trade works powerfully for peace and amity.

So far the discussion has related only to political union which was wholly peaceful and voluntary. But when Britain objected to customs union between Belgium and France in the 1840's, and when France objected to Austro-German customs union in 1931, as involving in each case a threat to the independence of the smaller country, what they undoubtedly had in mind was not so much the possibility that the Belgians or the Austrians, as the result of affection bred by close economic ties, would come to welcome fusion with the French, or the Germans, for its own sake. What they anticipated was rather that the economy of the smaller country would become so integrated with that of the larger that a sudden cutting of the ties would be unendurable, and that to avoid such a cutting it would have to accept whatever terms the larger country wished to impose upon it. Such at least has always been the argument in weak countries of opponents to specially close economic ties with strong and large neighboring countries.

The argument on its face certainly seems plausible, but there is not much historical evidence of a crucial sort which gives it direct support. Tiny states such as Monaco, Liechtenstein, Luxemburg, linked up in customs union with powerful neighbors, have preserved their political independence intact, perhaps because they were tiny, and Scotland, in the early eighteenth century, seems to be the only state, hitherto independent, to whose loss of independence economic coercion from outside made a significant and obvious contribution.

The Luxemburg case, however, even during its customs union with Prussia, may not be closely relevant. Luxemburg had friends outside, and its absorption by Germany would have been a *casus belli*.[22] Termination of the customs union with Germany, moreover, even sudden termination, would, as events have shown, not have been fatal for Luxemburg, since alternative economic partners, Belgium or France, were available to her. Liechtenstein also, despite its population of only 11,000, could live without Austrian partnership, while Monaco has

---

22. Luxemburg nevertheless was at least twice permitted to hear the Prussian saber rattle. On September 19, 1841, when Luxemburg was delaying ratification of the customs union with Prussia, Frederick William of Prussia warned William of Luxemburg that the opposition to customs union within Luxemburg came from the rebel French-Belgian party, and that it would lead to embroilment with the German states. In 1852, when Luxemburg had failed to reply to Prussian communications, it was told that Prussia "could not permit any state whatsoever to take her so lightly that it dares to treat official communications from her ministers as if they had never been received. Nor could she any longer tolerate on the part of Luxemburg that which, even if she did not have at her disposal 500,000 bayonets, she would not have endured for so long on the part of all the other four great powers of Europe acting in unison." Albert Calmes, *Der Zollanschluss des Grossherzogtums Luxemburg an Deutschland, 1842–1918*, [Luxemburg], 1919, I, 152; II, 45.

always supported itself by very special types of economic activity—piracy, smuggling, or public gambling—and absorption in a larger political unit would bring some measure of moral embarrassment to the heir to its sovereignty.[23]

The scarcity of positive supporting historical evidence, however, does not deprive of all its plausibility the argument that economic union between a small country and a large neighboring country carries with it an appreciable risk of loss of independence for the small country. Customs unions have not been formed at random, and many more have been proposed than have been consummated. Small countries, when they have any real freedom of choice, choose their economic partners with the greatest caution, and they stay out of customs unions with powerful neighbors unless there are present special circumstances which either free them from serious fears that their independence would in consequence be compromised or make this risk more acceptable than the more formidable risk that otherwise their independence would have to be surrendered to an even less welcome master. The case of Austria in 1931 would appear to be the only modern case where any country valuing its independence has nevertheless shown readiness to risk that independence for economic reasons, but Austria was acting from economic despair.

The power of nationalist sentiment can override all other considerations; it can dominate the minds of a people, and dictate the policies of government, even when in every possible way and to every conceivable degree it is in sharp conflict with what seem to be and are in fact the basic economic interests of the people in question. To accept as obviously true the notion that the bonds

23. If the capacity for survival as independent sovereignties of these miniscule principalities still calls for explanation, it seems to the writer that it must be sought in the traditional reluctance of respectable European states, even when they are themselves republics, completely to destroy by force the sovereignty of a long-established dynasty, especially when the gains would be small.

of allegiance must necessarily be largely economic in character to be strong, or to accept unhesitatingly the notion that where the economic entanglements are artificially or naturally strong the political affections will also necessarily become strong, is to reject whatever lessons past experience has for us in this field.

4. The Austro-German Treaty of 1918

The final outcome of the negotiations between Austria-Hungary and Germany during World War I for an "economic union," throws considerable light on the political and economic difficulties of forming customs unions where countries of comparable size and prestige are concerned.[24] There had been much talk in the Central Countries during the War about the formation of a "Mitteleuropa" with a unified tariff wall against the outside world and free trade within the union. When it came to the point of actual negotiation of such a union, however, unwillingness to surrender any of the important manifestations of sovereignty, reluctance to expose weak industries to unrestrained competition from other members of the union, and inability to agree on what third countries would be both willing and suitable partners, resulted in the emergence from the protracted negotiations of what was little more than a comprehensive reciprocity treaty between Germany and Austria-Hungary alone.

Neither country, apparently, and certainly not Austria-Hungary, wanted a complete customs union, but Germany did press for free trade between the member countries. To this Austria-Hungary would not consent, and in the final treaty, signed on October 11, 1918, at Salzburg after months of continuous negotiation, provision was made for the retention of

24. See *supra*, p. 88, for the early stages of these negotiations.

"intermediary duties" (*Zwischenzolle*) on several hundred tariff items covering about half the trade between the two countries. These were to be "provisional," and to be revised every five years in the direction of the lowering of the general level, but there was no definite commitment beyond this for their elimination. In general, as the principal negotiators for Austria-Hungary state in their account of the negotiations, "the determination of Austria-Hungary to protect her industries against the powerful competition of Germany is clearly apparent" in the agreement; whereas the German negotiators conceded almost complete free trade. They comment that "this, in fact, corresponded to the economic conditions and the competitive power of the two Empires," but it may reasonably be presumed that Germany regarded the agreement as a payment in economic terms for political gains.

On commodities made free of duty between the two countries, there was to be a uniform tariff on imports from outside countries, which could be changed only with the consent of both parties to the treaty. On commodities subject to internal duty by one of the countries (all commodities were made free of duty by one country or by both in trade between the two countries) there was, except for the provision that in both countries external duties should be levied which were higher than the intermediary duties, no such requirement, so as to "ensure greater freedom of action in negotiating commercial treaties with third States."

No provision was made for a common "Customs Parliament" or for common customs officials. "These were impossible for political reasons; and it was pointed out [presumably by the Austro-Hungarian negotiators] that they did not exist even inside the Austro-Hungarian Monarchy." It was agreed, however, that the customs laws and administration in both Empires should be "assimilated," and steps in this direction were taken. Permanent conferences were also to be established, "to supervise the application of the [uniform portion of the external?] tariff and of the Customs regulations." There was no real agreement on treaty relations with third countries.

Excise duties, whichever country they were levied in, were to be turned over to the country of consumption: "it was hoped to assimilate them as soon as possible."

The Austrian negotiators ended their account of the treaty with the following complacent comments:

> Thus, in the course of the negotiations there had been crystallized a simple formula which represents a new solution of the problem involved in the economic union of independent States. The problem is how such States can form an economic area, permitting the utmost possible freedom of movement within its limits and a common attitude towards the outside world, without surrendering their sovereign independence and without the ruin of important branches of their respective economic lives. To avoid this, the imperiled industries need for a long transition period protection against the competition of the allied States and also, as against other States, a larger measure of protection than the industries of the allied State. The problem is how to reconcile this with the development of freer intercourse within the alliance and with a common commercial policy.

They obviously believed that this treaty accomplished these purposes, although they conceded that without a common Customs Parliament "between several States such cooperation is impossible, owing to the too great complication of the machinery."[25]

---

25. This account is based on the account given by the two senior Austro-Hungarian negotiators, Gustav Gratz and Richard Schüller, in their work, *The Economic Policy of Austria-Hungary during the War in its External Relations* (1928), pp. 60–69, and all direct quotations are from this text. The original German version, *Die äussere Wirtschaftspolitik Österreich-Ungarns, Mitteleuropäische Pläne* (1925), pp. 93–100, gives the actual text of the main provisions of the treaty.

This treaty was negotiated when the Central Powers still expected either victory in the War or at least a stalemate. With their defeat, and the break-up of the Austro-Hungarian Empire, the treaty, of course, came to naught. A few comments on it may be offered. Even as a reciprocity treaty, it left several problems unsolved: harmony of relations with third countries; procedures for tariff revision; allocation of revenues from import duties collected in one country on goods destined for the other. It fell far short of a customs union, so that there was not the administrative economy resulting from the complete removal of a tariff wall. There was in the case of neither country, and especially not for Austria-Hungary, a real opening of its internal market to competition from low-cost industries in the other. All outside countries would have regarded the arrangements provided for by the treaty as in violation of the most-favored-nation principle, since in terms of the rules and interpretations then accepted it did not approximate sufficiently to a customs union to be exempt from them. The general lines of the arrangement, however, anticipate so fully those of later projects that it may be concluded either that it has served as a model or that the compromises reached are natural ones between countries of comparatively equal status when they wish to establish close economic relations but need not take the most-favored-nation principle seriously into account.

Chapter VI

The Havana Charter and Customs Union

1. The Most-Favored-Nation Principle

The Charter of the International Trade Organization which was drawn up at Havana, March 24, 1948,[1] at a conference of over fifty countries held under United Nations auspices, and which now awaits ratification by the participating countries, contains important provisions relating to customs unions. The Charter deals with a wide range of problems in the field of commercial policy. It lays down general principles or rules, as the case may be, to govern the commercial relations of adhering countries; it provides for a permanent international organization, with supervisory, advisory, and mandatory powers, to promote the application of these principles and rules, and, upon occasion, to sanction departures from them; and it requires adhering countries to engage in multilateral negotiations for the reduction or removal of existing trade barriers. Only such of its provisions as have close connection with the customs union question will be examined here.

The text of the Charter as it emerged from the Havana Conference was the product of a gradual process of elaboration and revision by international negotiation of an original draft charter prepared by experts on the staff of the American

1. *Havana Charter for an International Trade Organization, March 24, 1948*, U. S. Department of State, Commercial Policy Series 114.

Government and issued and circulated by the Department of State in September, 1946. The successive stages in this process of evolution are marked by four crucial documents: (1) the original American draft of September, 1946 ("Suggested Charter for an International Trade Organization of the United Nations") hereinafter to be cited as "Suggested Charter, 1946"; (2) the draft charter as revised at the London Meeting of the Preparatory Committee of the International Conference on Trade and Employment, October–November, 1946 ("Preliminary Draft, Charter for the International Trade Organization of the United Nations") hereinafter to be cited as "London Draft, 1946"; (3) the further-revised draft prepared at the Geneva Meeting of the Preparatory Committee of the United Nations Conference on Trade and Employment, April–August, 1947 ("Draft Charter for the International Trade Organization of the United Nations") hereinafter to be cited as "Geneva Draft, 1947"; and finally, (4) the Charter as revised at the United Nations Conference on Trade and Employment, Havana, November, 1947–March, 1948 ("Havana Charter for an International Trade Organization") hereinafter to be cited as "Havana Charter, 1948."[2] Where it will be serviceable in showing significant trends in the position taken by the participants in the drafting, comparisons will be made of these successive drafts.

The United States Government was the initiator and has continued to be the major sponsor of the Charter. Its main objectives, within the range of matters of special concern here, were three: to obtain rehabilitation and strengthening of the most-favored-nation principle, which since World War I, and

2. A "Lake Success Draft," an intermediate draft between the London and Geneva Drafts ("Report of the Drafting Committee of the Preparatory Committee of the United Nations Conference on Trade and Employment," Lake Success, New York, March, 1947), introduced no changes of consequence for present purposes, and need not therefore be considered here.

especially under the stress of the depression conditions prevailing during the 1930's, had undergone serious attrition in doctrine and still more in practical application; to promote the reduction of tariffs and the "elimination" of intra-imperial preferences through bilateral negotiations in a multilateral framework; to obtain as far as possible the abolition and renunciation of all official trade barriers other than ordinary import duties. In a few instances the American negotiators, in response to special interests of the United States—or perhaps more accurately, in response to pressures, actual or anticipated, from special interests in the United States—themselves advocated the sanctioning of departures from these objectives. In other instances they made concessions in advance or in the course of the negotiations to the demands of other countries for departures from these objectives. They were determined above all that a widely acceptable and workable Charter should emerge from the long and inevitably difficult negotiations. On the whole, however, the American negotiators supported, and supported tenaciously, all three objectives. Where the final Charter departs from them, or seriously compromises them, it must generally be attributed to the insistent demands of other countries to which the American negotiators felt obliged to make concessions if agreement was to be reached. There is no reason to believe that a "better" charter was obtainable.

The Havana Charter, 1948, lays down the unconditional most-favored-nation principle, with respect to import duties and to quantitative import restrictions, in two key paragraphs:

CHAPTER IV.—*Article 16*
1. With respect to customs duties and charges of any kind imposed on or in connection with importation or exportation or imposed on the international transfer of payments for imports or exports, and with respect to the method of levying

such duties and charges, and with respect to all rules and formalities in connection with importation and exportation, and with respect to all matters within the scope of paragraphs 2 and 4 of Article 18 [relating to internal taxes and internal regulations of commerce and transport], any advantage, favour, privilege or immunity granted by any Member to any product originating in or destined for any other country shall be accorded immediately and unconditionally to the like product originating in or destined for all other Member countries.

CHAPTER IV.—*Article 22*

1. No prohibition or restriction shall be applied by any Member on the importation of any product of any other Member country or on the exportation of any product destined for any other Member country, unless the importation of the like product of all third countries or the exportation of the like product to all third countries is similarly prohibited or restricted.

These are sufficiently rigorous provisions. Taken by themselves they not only carry on the traditional import of the most-favored-nation pledge, but they carry it forward in two respects: first, by making the rule of equality of treatment apply expressly to quantitative restrictions where formerly its applicability to them was implicit only and was frequently denied; secondly, by extending the application of the rule to the relations vis-à-vis outside countries of the different parts of a single "sovereign" country, if these parts have separate tariff regimes.[3] Except as specifically

3. This is achieved by Chapter IV, Article 42, which states that "Each... customs territory shall, exclusively for the purposes of the territorial application of Chapter IV, be treated as though it were a Member;" and, for the purposes of this chapter, defines "customs territory" as "any territory with respect to which separate tariffs or other regulations of commerce are maintained for a substantial part of the trade of such territory with other territories," but provides that the paragraph shall not be construed as creating any rights or obligations *inter se* for customs territories in respect of which the Charter has been accepted by a single Member.

exempted by the other provisions of the Charter, intra-imperial tariff relations are, for the first time in history in an international document, it is believed, declared to be within the scope of the most-favored-nation principle.[4] There are elsewhere provided, it is true, important exceptions from the equality-of-treatment rule for *existing* preferences, intra-imperial, or otherwise, but political relationships—short, presumably, of complete legislative union—are not given any weight with respect to *new* preferences not specifically provided for in the Charter.

2. Exemptions from Most-Favored-Nations Obligations of Customs Unions, Free-Trade Areas, and Interim Agreements

Article 44 of the Havana Charter, 1948, deals specifically with customs unions, "free-trade areas," and interim agreements leading to the formation of customs unions or of free-trade areas. The text of the article, with portions added at some stage subsequent to the issue of the Suggested Charter, 1946, marked off by square brackets, follows. The annotations either indicate the time of first appearance of the text here placed within square brackets, or provide explanatory material.

ARTICLE 44

[1. Members recognize the desirability of increasing freedom of trade by the development, through voluntary agreements,

---

4. "Open-door" clauses with respect to colonies have the same effect, but were never treated as integral parts of the most-favored-nation provision. "Nation" was invariably interpreted to mean a politically sovereign unit. When a mother country in the nineteenth century pledged itself to establish equal treatment for all imports into its colonies whatever their source or for all imports into the metropolitan area whatever their source, it always did so in express language and never as automatically taken care of by the standard most-favored-nation clause.

of closer integration between the economies of the countries parties to such agreements. They also recognize that the purpose of a customs union or free-trade area should be to facilitate trade between the parties and not to raise barriers to the trade of other Member countries with such parties.][5]

2. Accordingly, the provisions of this Chapter shall not prevent [, as between the territories of Members,][6] the formation of a customs union [or of a free-trade area or the adoption of an interim agreement necessary for the formation of a customs union or of a free-trade area;][7] *Provided* that:

(*a*) with respect to a customs union, [or an interim agreement leading to the formation of a customs union,] the duties and other regulations of commerce imposed at the institution of any such union [or interim agreement] in respect of trade with Member countries not parties to such union [or agreement] shall not on the whole be higher or more restrictive than the [general incidence][8] of the duties and regulations of commerce applicable in the constituent territories prior to the formation of such union [or the adoption of such interim agreement, as the case may be];

[(*b*) with respect to a free-trade area, or an interim agreement leading to the formation of a free-trade area, the duties and other regulations of commerce maintained in each of

5. First appearance in the Havana Charter, 1948.

6. Introduced in Havana Charter, 1948. The new phrase is presumably intended to protect Article 98, paragraph 3, which permits customs unions, etc., with non-members of the I. T. O. only when approved by a two-thirds vote of the Organization.

7. All references to "free-trade area" in the Charter made their first appearance in Havana Charter, 1948. References to "interim agreements" in the Charter made their first appearance in Geneva Draft, 1947.

8. Until the Havana Charter, 1948, instead of "general incidence" the texts read "average level." Both terms have about equal uncertainty of meaning. The phrase in 2 (*a*) "on the whole" apparently means, with respect to the customs union area as

the constituent territories and applicable at the formation of such free-trade area or the adoption of such interim agreement to the trade of Member countries not included in such area or not parties to such agreement shall not be higher or more restrictive than the corresponding duties and other regulations of commerce existing in the same constituent territories prior to the formation of the free-trade area, or interim agreement, as the case may be; and

(c) any interim agreement referred to in sub-paragraphs (a) or (b) shall include a plan and schedule for the formation of such a custom union or of such a free-trade area within a reasonable length of time.][9]

3. (a) Any Member deciding to enter into a customs union [or free-trade area, or an interim agreement leading to the formation of such a union or area,] shall promptly notify[10] the Organization and shall make available to it such information regarding the proposed union or area as will enable the Organization to make such reports and recommendations to Members as it may deem appropriate.

[(b) If, after having studied the plan and schedule provided for in an interim agreement referred to in paragraph 2 in consultation with the parties to that agreement and taking due account of the information made available in accordance with the provisions of sub-paragraph (a), the Organization finds that such agreement is not likely to result in the formation of a customs union or of a free-trade area within the period contemplated by the parties to the agreement or that

---

a whole. Free-trade areas are made subject to a more restrictive requirement. See 2 (b), and *infra*, p. 124, for further comment on this point.

9. Introduced in Havana Charter, 1948.

10. Until the Havana Charter, 1948, the texts read "shall consult with" instead of "shall promptly notify."

such period is not a reasonable one, the Organization shall make recommendations to the parties to the agreement. The parties shall not maintain or put into force, as the case may be, such agreement if they are not prepared to modify it in accordance with these recommendations.][11]

[(c) Any substantial change in the plan or schedule referred to in paragraph 2(c) shall be communicated to the Organization, which may request the Members concerned to consult with it if the change seems likely to jeopardize or delay unduly the formation of the customs union or of the free-trade area.][12]

4. For the purposes of this Charter:

(a) a customs union shall be understood to mean the substitution of a single customs territory for two or more customs territories, so that

(i) duties and other restrictive regulations of commerce [except, where necessary, those permitted under Section B of Chapter IV[13] and under Article 45][14] are eliminated with respect to

---

11. In the Geneva Draft, 1947, the corresponding subparagraph, which then made its first appearance, referred only to interim agreements preparatory to customs unions, and read as follows:

"(b) No Member shall institute or maintain any interim agreement... if, after a study of the plan and schedule proposed in such agreement, the Organization finds that such agreement is not likely to result in such a customs union within a reasonable length of time."

12. In the Geneva Charter, 1947, the corresponding subparagraph, which then made its first appearance, read:

"(c) The plan or schedule shall not be substantially altered without consultation with the Organization."

13. These are limited rights to maintain quantitative restrictions on imports in connection with agricultural stabilization programs, to cope with balance of payments difficulties, etc.

14. These relate to import and export prohibitions or restrictions on moral or sanitary grounds, in the interest of conservation, in connection with domestic price controls, etc.

substantially all the trade between the constituent territories of the union [or at least with respect to substantially all the trade in products originating in such territories,][15] and,

(ii)[subject to the provisions of paragraph 5,][16] [substantially][17] the same duties and other regulations of commerce are applied by each of the members of the union to the trade of territories not included in the union;

[(b) a free-trade area shall be understood to mean a group of two or more customs territories in which the duties and other restrictive regulations of commerce (except, where necessary, those permitted under Section B of Chapter IV and under Article 45)[18] are eliminated on substantially all the trade between the constituent territories in products originating in such territories.][19]

[5. The preferences referred to in paragraph 2 of Article 16 shall not be affected by the formation of a customs union or of a free-trade area but may be eliminated or adjusted by means of negotiations with Members affected. This procedure of negotiations with affected Members shall, in particular, apply to the elimination of preferences required to conform with the provisions of paragraph 4(a) (i) and paragraph 4(b).][20]

---

15. This relaxation of the requirement as to elimination of tariffs, etc., within the customs union with respect to products not originating within the union was first introduced in the Havana Charter. Since the definition of a "customs union" given in 4(a) of this article does not include the requirement of allocation of customs revenues among members by formula, a customs union set up without provision for such allocation would need the benefit of this relaxation unless it was prepared to accept assignment of revenues according to place of collection. See *supra,* pp. 78 ff.

16. Inserted in the Havana Charter, 1948.

17. Inserted in the Geneva Draft, 1947.

18. See p. 114, notes 13 and 14, *supra.*

19. Inserted in the Havana Charter, 1948.

20. This paragraph was first introduced in the Havana Charter, 1948. Its purpose is to permit the coordination of the provisions of Article 44 with the provisions in the

[6. The Organization may, by a two-thirds majority of the Members present and voting, approve proposals which do not fully comply with the requirements of the preceding paragraphs, provided that such proposals lead to the formation of a customs union or of a free-trade area in the sense of this Article.][21]

3. Exemptions from Most-Favored-Nation Obligations of Agreements in the Interest of Economic Development, Including Regional Agreements

The London Draft, 1946, was the first to contain provisions dealing with "Economic Development," but these made no express reference to international tariff arrangements or to most-favored-nation obligations. The Geneva Draft, 1947,

Charter sanctioning all existing preferential arrangements, but requiring the countries involved to negotiate with other countries for their reduction. Upon American insistence, reductions of preferences are always referred to in the Charter as the "elimination" or "measures directed to the elimination" of preferences.

21. This paragraph first appeared in the Havana Charter, 1948, but it has an interesting and significant history.

(1) The London Draft Charter, 1946, contained, in the article dealing with Customs Union, the following paragraph:

"The Members recognize that there may in exceptional circumstances be justification for new preferential arrangements requiring an exception to the provisions of [the chapter dealing with Customs Unions]. Any such exception shall be subject to approval by [a two-thirds majority of] the Organization."

(2) In the Geneva Draft, 1947, the customs union provisions were relaxed by the extension of the exemption from most-favored nation obligations to "interim agreements necessary for the attainment of a customs union." This was presumably regarded as providing sufficient freedom for arrangements aiming at but not immediately achieving customs union, and the

contained the paragraph just cited[22] authorizing the Organization to approve, by two-thirds majority vote, special exemption from most-favored-nation obligations for preferential arrangements between two or more countries in the interest of "economic development"; and an additional paragraph which has not been reproduced here laid down the procedure required to obtain approval by the Organization. The Havana Charter retains these paragraphs, including the requirement of approval by a two-thirds majority vote, but it adds an additional category of

paragraph just quoted from the London Draft Charter was dropped out of the Customs Union article but placed instead, with a significant change, in a new chapter dealing with "Economic Development." The new feature introduced was that the release from most-favored-nation obligations was now made available to international arrangements in the interest of "economic development" even though customs union was not contemplated. The article as it appeared in the Geneva Draft (but omitting the paragraph prescribing procedure for, obtaining International Trade Organization approval) was as follows:

"1. The Members recognize that special circumstances may justify new preferential arrangements between two or more countries, not contemplating a customs union, in the interest of the programmes of economic development or reconstruction of one or more such countries. Subject to such limitations as it may impose, the Organization may grant [by an affirmative vote of two-thirds of the Members voting] an exception to the provisions of Chapter IV to permit such arrangements to be made."

The square brackets appear in the original text, and are not explained. A note to the article as a whole, however, states that the delegates of Brazil and Chile entered reservations with respect to the voting requirements, and this may explain the square brackets, although reservations to other sections of the Geneva Draft are not similarly treated. In the Geneva Draft, 1947, as in the Havana Charter, 1948, Chapter IV was the chapter containing the general provisions requiring adherence to the most-favored-nation principle.

(3) In the Havana Charter, 1948, this article received further elaboration and became chiefly an article relaxing most-favored-nation obligations for regional agreements. (Article 15.) Its text is given *infra,* pp. 117 ff.

22. *Supra,* note 21.

arrangements, "regional preferential agreements," which are to be entitled to exemption from most-favored-nation obligations. This marks the first appearance in the evolution of the Charter of express recognition of "regional agreements."

The text of the relevant article in the Havana Charter, 1948, is as follows:

ARTICLE 15.—*Preferential Agreements for Economic Development and Reconstruction*

1. The Members recognize that special circumstances, including the need for economic development or reconstruction, may justify new preferential agreements between two or more countries in the interest of the programmes of economic development or reconstruction of one or more of them.

2. Any Member contemplating the conclusion of such an agreement shall communicate its intention to the Organization and provide it with the relevant information to enable it to examine the proposed agreement. The Organization shall promptly communicate such information to all Members.

3. The Organization shall examine the proposal and, by a two-thirds majority of the Members present and voting, may grant, subject to such conditions as it may impose, an exception to the provisions of Article 16[23] to permit the proposed agreement to become effective.

4. Notwithstanding the provisions of paragraph 3, the Organization shall authorize, in accordance with the provisions of paragraphs 5 and 6, the necessary departure from the provisions of Article 16 in respect of a proposed

---

23. Article 16 is the general provision requiring adherence to the most-favored-nation principle, but exempting from this requirement existing preferential arrangements.

agreement between Members for the establishment of tariff preferences which it determines to fulfil the following conditions and requirements:

(*a*) the territories of the parties to the agreement are contiguous one with another, or all parties belong to the same economic region;

(*b*) any preference provided for in the agreement is necessary to ensure a sound and adequate market for a particular industry or branch of agriculture which is being, or is to be, created or reconstructed or substantially developed or substantially modernized;

(*c*) the parties to the agreement undertake to grant free entry for the products of the industry or branch of agriculture referred to in sub-paragraph (*b*) or to apply customs duties to such products sufficiently low to ensure that the objectives set forth in that sub-paragraph will be achieved;

(*d*) any compensation granted to the other parties by the party receiving preferential treatment shall, if it is a preferential concession, conform with the provisions of this paragraph;

(*e*) the agreement contains provisions permitting, on terms and conditions to be determined by negotiation with the parties to the agreement, the adherence of other Members, which are able to qualify as parties to the agreement under the provisions of this paragraph, in the interest of their programmes of economic development or reconstruction. The provisions of Chapter VIII[24] may be invoked by such a Member in this respect only on the ground that it has been unjustifiably excluded from participation in such an agreement;

---

24. Chapter VIII provides procedures whereby a member which considers that any benefit to which it is entitled under the provisions of the Charter (except Article 1, whose "preambular" nature thus receives a degree of recognition perhaps unique in legislative documents) is being nullified or impaired in any way can seek redress.

(*f*) the agreement contains provisions for its termination within a period necessary for the fulfilment of its purposes but, in any case, not later than at the end of ten years; any renewal shall be subject to the approval of the Organization and no renewal shall be for a longer period than five years.

5. When the Organization, upon the application of a Member and in accordance with the provisions of paragraph 6, approves a margin of preference as an exception to Article 16[25] in respect of the products covered by the proposed agreement, it may, as a condition of its approval, require a reduction in an unbound most-favoured-nation rate of duty proposed by the Member in respect of any product so covered, if in the light of the representations of any affected Member it considers that rate excessive.

6. (*a*) If the Organization finds that the proposed agreement fulfils the conditions and requirements set forth in paragraph 4 and that the conclusion of the agreement is not likely to cause substantial injury to the external trade of a Member country not party to the agreement, it shall within two months authorize the parties to the agreement to depart from the provisions of Article 16, as regards the products covered by the agreement. If the Organization does not give a ruling within the specified period, its authorization shall be regarded as having been automatically granted.

(*b*) If the Organization finds that the proposed agreement, while fulfilling the conditions and requirements set forth in paragraph 4, is likely to cause substantial injury to the external trade of a Member country not party to the agreement, it shall inform interested Members of its findings and shall require the Members contemplating the conclusion of the agreement to enter into negotiations with that

25. See note 23, p. 117, *supra*.

Member. When agreement is reached in the negotiations, the Organization shall authorize the Members contemplating the conclusion of the preferential agreement to depart from the provisions of Article 16 as regards the products covered by the preferential agreement. If, at the end of two months from the date on which the Organization suggested such negotiations, the negotiations have not been completed and the Organization considers that the injured Member is unreasonably preventing the conclusion of the negotiations, it shall authorize the necessary departure from the provisions of Article 16 and at the same time shall fix a fair compensation to be granted by the parties to the agreement to the injured Member or, if this is not possible or reasonable, prescribe such modification of the agreement as will give such Member fair treatment. The provisions of Chapter VIII[26] may be invoked by such Member only if it does not accept the decision of the Organization regarding such compensation.

(c) If the Organization finds that the proposed agreement, while fulfilling the conditions and requirements set forth in paragraph 4, is likely to jeopardize the economic position of a Member in world trade, it shall not authorize any departure from the provisions of Article 16 unless the parties to the agreement have reached a mutually satisfactory understanding with that Member.

(d) If the Organization finds that the prospective parties to a regional preferential agreement have, prior to November 21, 1947, obtained from countries representing at least two-thirds of their import trade the right to depart from most-favoured-nation treatment in the cases envisaged in the agreement, the Organization shall, without prejudice to the conditions governing the recognition of such right,

26. See note 24, p. 118, *supra*.

grant the authorization provided for in paragraph 5 and in sub-paragraph (*a*) of this paragraph, provided that the conditions and requirements set out in sub-paragraphs (*a*), (*e*) and (*f*) of paragraph 4 are fulfilled. Nevertheless, if the Organization finds that the external trade of one or more Member countries, which have not recognized this right to depart from most-favoured-nation treatment, is threatened with substantial injury, it shall invite the parties to the agreement to enter into negotiations with the injured Member, and the provisions of sub-paragraph (*b*) of this paragraph shall apply.

4. Relations with Non-Members

The Havana Charter expressly authorizes (Article 98, paragraph 3) members to enter into arrangements with non-members for customs unions, interim agreements leading to customs unions, free-trade areas, regional agreements, and special preferential arrangements, but it makes *all* such arrangements, if they include non-members, subject to approval by a two-thirds majority vote of the Organization.

A provision of the Charter (paragraph 2 [*b*] of Article 98) requires that, subject to certain qualifications apparently not relevant here, "no Member shall accord to the trade of any non-Member country treatment which, being more favourable than that which it accords to the trade of any other Member country, would injure the economic interests of a Member country." This raises the interesting, and potentially important, question as to what the situation would be if a non-member country having a treaty with a member country containing an unqualified most-favored-nation pledge were to demand the extension to it

of the concessions which the member country had made to other
treaty countries by virtue, say, of a preferential regional agreement. There would here appear to be a conflict of legal obligations for the member country.

5. Significance of the Havana Charter for the Customs Union Question

The significance of the Havana Charter is not confined to those
provisions of the Charter which have been examined here. In so
far as the operation of the Charter, and especially the multilateral
reduction or elimination of trade barriers, results in less feeling of
dissatisfaction with their international economic status on the part
of member countries, there will be less interest in customs union
as a possible means of relieving economic strains and promoting
national prosperity. The Havana Charter gives verbal encouragement to the formation of customs unions, and by freeing them
from most-favored-nation obligations even when they are in an
interim stage it facilitates their establishment.

The Havana Charter places in the same category with perfect or complete customs unions, with respect to freedom from
most-favored-nation obligations, customs unions which are only
partial. In its definition of "customs union," it makes no mention of an agreed formula for allocation of customs revenue, or
of merging or sharing in common the customs administration of
the union. All that the Charter requires to constitute a "customs
union" is that each member territory shall have substantially the
same set of trade barriers as against countries outside the union,
and that substantially all the trade between the members of the
union be free of restrictions, and this last is further qualified so
that it need apply only to the trade in products originating within
the union.

Until the Havana Charter, 1948, the successive drafts of the Charter gave no encouragement to preferential arrangements based on political ties, or on sentimental considerations, or on free choice of the participants,[27] or on contiguity of the participants or their location in the same "region," presumably in deference to American attitudes.

There are good grounds on which special objections may be based against intra-imperial preferences. First, as far as economic considerations are concerned, the selection of partners for the arrangements tends to be wholly fortuitous, the result of historical accident. Second, the arrangements are likely to be not the results of bargaining at arms' length—aided perhaps by sentiments of mutual good-will—but to be imposed on the colonial partners by the mother country. In some instances this means arrangements specially generous to the colonies, whether intentionally so or not—as in the case, for example, of the relations between continental United States and Hawaii, or between Britain and its sugar-growing colonies—but it probably more often, and certainly often, tends to mean that the arrangement involves exploitation of a defenseless colonial people by the country with sovereign power over it.

While existing intra-imperial preferences are given sanction by the Havana Charter as under all the preceding Drafts, the extension or the establishment of new ones is disallowed unless these are covered by provisions of the Charter permitting preferential arrangements on other grounds than political ties, and existing intra-imperial preferences are made subject to "elimination" through the process of mutual bargaining to reduce trade

---

27. Perhaps this should be qualified by reference to the authorization of special preferential arrangements in the interest of economic development or reconstruction, which are not otherwise expressly limited in their scope. But these were subject to the stiff requirement of prior approval by the Organization by a two-thirds majority vote.

barriers which members of the International Trade Organization are required to engage in under the Charter.

There was introduced into the Havana Charter, 1948, however, an elaborate provision sanctioning preferential regional agreements. In the past regional agreements were exempt from most-favored-nation obligations only by express stipulation and with reference to specified countries or "regions." In the Havana Charter they receive a general sanction, but subject to conditions of an economic character which may prove in practice difficult to meet if they are strictly enforced. The provisions of the Charter with respect to regional agreements appear to reflect the ideas behind the Latin-American agreements commented on in an earlier section,[28] and to be frankly designed to permit the area of effective protection of high-cost industries to be extended beyond the boundaries of a single country. These countries need not be "contiguous," but if not contiguous they must be in "the same economic region," whatever that may mean. But the limited duration permitted for such agreements and the sanction of preference only when it "is necessary to assure a sound and adequate market" indicate that the intent is to cover only protection of the "infant industry" or "development" type.

It is not evident that contiguity or proximity has sufficient economic significance of itself to justify special sanction for tariff preferences on that score, especially if the preferential arrangements do not go the full length of customs union and therefore do not result in the elimination of tariff walls. The Economic Committee of the League of Nations in 1936 commented that "the haphazard formation of fresh groups of neighbouring countries having no special historical or economic association would, it must be recognised, tend progressively to deprive the

28. See *supra*, p. 20.

most-favoured-nation clause of its value."[29] This seems to be a sound proposition.[30] If there is an economic case for specially close economic ties between two or more territories, the case is likely to be stronger if it is made to rest on specifically economic criteria than on such largely fortuitous factors as proximity. In the early history of the American Presbyterian Church there was much discussion as to the relative merits of "propinquity" and "elective affinity" as bases for affiliations between congregations. In sanctioning preferential tariff arrangements, there is much to be said for "elective affinity" if based on reasonable economic considerations as against the accidents of geography or political history.[31]

The case is even stronger against special preferential arrangements between countries within "the same economic region" but without specific requirement of contiguity, unless the freedom of association this gives is used to establish arrangements which do have economic justification but would not come under any of the categories of preferential arrangements expressly formulated by the Charter as providing valid claims to exemption from most-favored-nation obligations without being subject to the requirement of approval by a two-thirds majority vote of the

29. League of Nations, Economic Committee, *Equality of Treatment in the Present State of International Commercial Relations,* Geneva, 1936 (Document C.379.M.250.1936. II.B.), p. 23.

30. Though not so the Economic Committee's approval of intra-imperial preferences and of "regional exceptions based on long-standing historical ... associations," unless the approval rested merely on the political necessity of accepting long- and firmly-established institutions, or on recognition that preferential arrangements of long standing cannot without economic shock be suddenly terminated. On purely economic grounds, such groupings are likely to be at least as "haphazard" as new regional groupings.

31. Cf. Pitman B. Potter, "Universalism versus Regionalism in International Organization," *American Political Science Review,* XXXVII (1943), 858: "The basic idea of regionalism is open to two serious objections: neighboring nations are not always logical or actual coöperators, which distant nations often are."

Organization. Economists have claimed to find use in the concept of an "economic region," but it cannot be said that they have succeeded in finding a definition of it which would be of much aid to the Organization in deciding whether two or more territories were in the same economic region.[32] For the purposes which the concept has been made by economists to serve, moreover, the stress is on complementarity of the territories within the region, whereas it has been argued here that it is a certain kind of economic rivalry between the territories, rivalry in the production of commodities whose unit-cost of production is low in one of the territories and high in the other or others, which makes preferential removal of trade barriers between the territories constitute a movement in the direction of a better international allocation of productive resources where the alternative is no removal at all of trade barriers. A preferential arrangement between two countries not contiguous to each other, whether or not they are in the same "region," moreover, cannot make any significant contribution to the reduction of the administrative costs of tariff barriers.

The Charter also exempts, from most-favored-nation obligations the relations between the members of a "free-trade area." This term is introduced, as a technical term, into the language of this field by the Charter, and its meaning for the purposes of the Charter must therefore be sought wholly within the text of the Charter. But the only requirement stipulated by the Charter, if an arrangement is to constitute a "free-trade area," is that trade barriers have been eliminated with respect to substantially all the trade between the customs territories of the area in products originating in such territories. This is also one of the requirements

---

32. On the difficulties of defining an "economic region," see Joseph J. Spengler, "Regional Differences and the Future of Manufacturing in America," *Southern Economic Journal*, VII (1941), 475–81.

of a customs union, whether as traditionally defined or as more broadly defined in the Charter. As far as the type of institution is concerned, therefore, countries wishing to free their trade relations with each other from most-favored-nation obligations need not proceed to the customs union stage. If a regional agreement is not appropriate, they can establish a free-trade area. In the case, however, of both regional agreements and free-trade areas, the Charter grants less freedom with respect to degree of barrier against imports from outside the area than in the case of customs unions. For customs unions, for example, the restrictions on imports from outside must not be higher "on the whole" for the area as a whole, whereas for a free-trade area they must not be higher for *each* of the member countries.

The major difference between a "free-trade area" and a "customs union" as both are defined in the Charter is that the former need not, and the latter must, have a uniform tariff as against imports from outside countries. What economic significance this would have in practice it is difficult to say. As compared to customs union, it might mean either that the low-tariff member of a free-trade area need not raise its tariff to meet the demands of a high-tariff partner, or that a high-tariff member need not lower its tariff to meet the demands of a low-tariff partner. But free-trade areas would present some special difficulties from which complete customs unions would be free. One such problem would be how to prevent one member country from selling to the other the output of a protected high-cost industry while supplying its own consumption by import from abroad, with the import duties going to its own treasury.

There might be important *political* significance, however, in the difference between a complete customs union and a "free-trade area," especially if one of the members was much larger than the other. Since the members of the latter could, in theory at least, have different tariff policies toward outside countries, and would have to maintain the tariff wall between themselves in order to guard against the entrance free-of-duty of dutiable goods originating in outside countries, there would be less call for common tariff policies and for unified customs administration and less pressure on the smaller country, therefore, to conform to the legislation of the larger.[33]

The relaxation of most-favored-nation obligations for interim agreements leading to the formation of customs unions or of free-trade areas is logical once customs unions and free-trade areas are accepted as desirable. Under modern conditions, the sudden removal of trade barriers as between two or more countries can involve great shock and disturbance to the economies involved, and if there was to be encouragement to the formation of customs unions and allied arrangements, it was only sensible to extend this encouragement also to the gradual movement towards these objectives which under present conditions is an essential prerequisite to the attainment of these objectives.[34]

Of a type of tariff arrangement which for a time seemed to be enthusiastically supported by the United States, the "plurilateral agreement," there is no express recognition in the Charter; and the only recognition in the Charter, even by implication, that the larger the number of countries participating in a preferential arrangement, other things equal, the less undesirable— or the more desirable—it is, lies in the condition, with respect to a regional agreement entitled to automatic authorization by

33. Cf. Wallace Goforth, "Canada's Economic Future," *International Journal* (Quarterly of the Canadian Institute of International Affairs), III (1948), 285–308. A full-fledged customs union between the United States and Canada is rejected, as involving the loss of Canada's political independence (pp. 294 and 308). A "Free Trade Area" is, however, found acceptable from the Canadian point of view, as "in effect,...another and somewhat more effective form of 'Reciprocity Treaty,' which Canada has often considered, and once actually enjoyed during the middle years of the nineteenth century." (Pp. 295–307.)

34. See *Customs Unions, 1947,* "Gradual Adjustment of Tariff," pp. 89–91.

the Organization, that "the agreement contains provisions permitting, on terms and conditions to be determined by negotiation with the parties to the agreement, the adherence of other Members." This condition is substantially a weak form of the *conditional* most-favored-nation pledge, which proved even in less weak forms to be of no value to countries invoking it to obtain equality of treatment. The larger the number of countries participating in a preferential tariff arrangement, the more likely it is that it will contribute more to removal of barriers to international specialization of production than to their intensification.[35] It is to be regretted, therefore, that as effective provisions as could be formulated for open entry on genuinely equal terms were not prescribed as a condition to be met by all projects for preferential arrangements if they were to be given exemption from most-favored-nation obligations.

In so far as escape from most-favored-nation obligations has been a major reason why countries seeking closer economic relations with each other choose or consider the customs union type of arrangement, the Havana Charter, by its extension to free-trade areas and regional agreements, as well as to partial customs unions, of exemption from most-favored-nation obligations, will operate to make these other types of arrangements more attractive than hitherto, *as compared to customs unions.* On the other hand, in so far as the Charter and the International Trade Organization succeed in bringing about a general reduction in trade barriers and other ameliorations of international economic relations, they will operate to reduce the incentives to enter into *any kind* of preferential tariff arrangement.

In the course of its evolution, the text of the Charter has thus accumulated an impressive list of types of preferential

---

35. See *supra,* p. 51.

tariff arrangements which are to be entitled to exemption from most-favored-nation obligations in so far as the trade relations between the participants therein are concerned. It is sometimes claimed on behalf of the Charter, in effect, that only those of its provisions which support and strengthen the most-favored-nation principle are entitled to emphasis, since whatever relaxations from the principle the Charter sanctions either have been widely prevalent in practice in the past or were destined to be so in the future even in the absence of the Charter. There is partial, but only partial, validity in this argument.

In the past, the only effective sanctions for adherence to the most-favored-nation principle were the advantages seen in such adherence. The pledges to grant such treatment were given voluntarily and were terminable. More equality of treatment prevailed without reference to pledges than was governed by pledges. The *granting* of most-favored-nation treatment may at times and for some countries have seemed burdensome, but assurance of *receiving* it, at least as a minimum, has always been valued, and departure from the former carried with it the risk or the certainty of losing the latter. When the Charter approves departures from the most-favored-nation principle, the significance of this approval does not lie merely in that it gives the odor of sanctity to practices which, whether widely followed or not, were hitherto not in good repute, although its significance even on this score is by no means negligible. What is of greater significance is that when the Charter gives its approval to a departure from the principle of most-favored-nation treatment, it at the same time assures to the countries who take advantage of it that they will not in consequence have to pay any price for their exercise of the privilege in the form of the loss of any claims they may have, legal or otherwise, to the receipt of most-favored-nation treatment from other countries. The fear of retaliation, or of counter-measures of some sort, has always been the most effective of all barriers to official discrimination in the treatment of international trade; where the Charter prohibits discrimination, it greatly strengthens the force of that barrier; where it sanctions discrimination, it removes it wholly or substantially. The provisions of the Charter with respect to customs unions, free-trade areas, and new regional agreements, *taken by themselves,* do constitute what is on paper at least an appreciable removal of preexisting barriers to official discrimination in trade barriers, and it is significant that many of these provisions are written in terms of hearty encouragement rather than of regrettable departure from an ideal made necessary by special circumstances or by the less-than-universal acceptance of the ideal. It should be conceded, however, that much can be said in support of the preferability of a code, even if imperfect, enforced by international sanction to an even better code enforced only by the sanctions of the possibility of unilateral national retaliation.

Chapter VII

Prospects for Customs Unions

1. Customs Unions Now in Operation or in Active Process of Negotiation

As far as available information goes, some twelve pre-World-War-II customs unions, all of them "complete" ones or substantially so, have survived the war, or have been successfully reestablished. The countries involved are as follows: France-Monaco; Italy–San Marino; Nigeria–British Cameroons; British Togoland–Gold Coast; Union of South Africa–Southern Rhodesia; Union of South Africa–Northern Rhodesia; Switzerland-Liechtenstein; Belgium-Luxemburg; Belgian Congo–Ruanda–Urundi; Tanganyika-Kenya-Uganda; Northern Rhodesia–Southern Rhodesia; Syria-Lebanon. In addition, Benelux has come into limited operation, Franco-Italian negotiations are making progress, and Colombia, Ecuador, Panama, and Venezuela ("Gran-Colombia") have set up an international organization to formulate proposals for closer economic union going beyond the limits sanctioned by the Havana Charter.[1]

Of these fifteen unions, at least four, those in which Liechtenstein, Luxemburg (with reference to the Belgium-Luxemburg customs

---

1. *New York Times,* April 23, 1949, p. 5. See also the "Quito Charter," an Agreement with a View to the Establishment of a Greater Colombia Economic and Customs Union (Pan American Union, Division of Conferences and Organizations; mimeographed text), and *supra,* p. 39.

union), Monaco, and San Marino are members, are customs unions between tiny sovereign states, on the one hand, and larger neighbors on the other. These customs unions are obviously unimportant except to their lesser members. Seven others of these unions in the list are between African countries; the members are Belgian colonies, British colonies, or British colonies and the Union of South Africa. Their economic importance is small. In most cases their *raison d'être* is mainly economy in the collection of import duties levied chiefly for purposes of revenue, although the desire for an enlarged market in which domestic industries can receive tariff protection is a factor in several of them. One other, Syria-Lebanon, is probably also mainly fiscal in its significance, with customs union resorted to chiefly as an economic method of collecting taxes. How far the Gran-Colombia union will go it is too early to forecast, but the nature of the economies of the member countries—the absence of important industries operating under tariff protection, the similarity of their major export products, the absence of any important basis for the development of trade between them whether in high-cost or in low-cost products—means that the union is likely to have only moderate significance for its members and very minor significance for the outside world regardless of its terms.

Of all of these actual or prospective customs unions, only Benelux and France-Italy have more than one member of industrial (manufacturing) and commercial importance. Benelux is still to come into full operation; up to the present important quantitative restrictions on trade between the members are still enforced, as are revenue duties, and, as we have seen, cartel agreements are relied upon to restrain competition between the industries of the member countries. The Franco-Italian customs union still has many hurdles to surmount before it can come into even partial operation. If customs union is to be an important phenomenon for the post-World-War-II world, the importance, therefore, must derive from customs unions still to be initiated or completed.

2. Customs Union in Western Europe

Since before the end of World War II, discussion of a customs union, or of a series of customs unions, to embrace all or most of Western Europe has been widespread, British participation therein being contemplated by some, while others believe that, aside from other reasons, Britain's relations with the Dominions and with the Sterling Area will make her reluctant to tie up too closely with the Continent as well as create insuperable obstacles on both sides to her entrance into customs union with Continental countries which find themselves in competition with Dominion agricultural production.

The American program of European Aid has ever since the launching of the "Marshall Plan" served to stimulate discussion and study of the possibilities of customs union in Western Europe, and the development of the political rift between Western and Eastern Europe has further accentuated it and given it marked political and strategic overtones. One of the conditions on which American aid is being granted is that the beneficiary countries pursue economic recovery through self-help on a collaborative basis, and it has been made clear that the United States Government would welcome political as well as economic unification of Western Europe, in part or in whole. As part of this program, "customs union," small or large, partial or complete, is being given steady encouragement.

In the presentation of their case for the receipt of American aid, the participating European countries bound themselves collectively:

(i) to abolish as soon as possible the abnormal restrictions which at present hamper their mutual trade;

(ii) to aim, as between themselves and the rest of the world, at a sound and balanced multilateral trading system based on the principles which have guided the framers of the Draft Charter for an International Trade Organization.[2]

The Havana Charter offers a general welcome to the formation of customs union, and the European Committee could not but be aware that in the prevailing state of mind in the United States there would be special welcome for any move on their part in the direction of customs union, which would be regarded as a notable manifestation of their will to recovery through mutual economic collaboration. In part at least in response to their interpretation of American wishes, the European Committee, in its Report, gave considerable attention to the question of customs union.[3]

The Committee expounds, in familiar terms, the advantages of the formation of a larger free-trade area in Europe. It draws attention, however, to some of the obstacles to the negotiation of customs union, and stresses the necessity of making progress slowly. It makes no promises, but points to the negotiation of Benelux, to scheduled meetings of the Scandinavian countries for the purpose of canvassing the possibilities of forming a Scandinavian customs union,[4] to the establishment by thirteen participating countries[5] of a "Study Group" to consider the problems involved for countries wishing to form a customs union, and to the formation by France and Italy of a smaller study group to consider a Franco-Italian customs union. The Report gives the text of a declaration by the French Government, with which the

2. Committee of European Economic Co-operation, *General Report,* Paris, September 21, 1947 (U. S. Department of State Publication 2930), I, 30.

3. See *ibid.,* I, 33–37.

4. On November 3, 1949, Denmark, Norway, and Sweden announced their intention of taking prompt action toward forming a customs union. *New York Times,* November 4, 1949. The negotiations have since collapsed.

5. Norway, Sweden, and Switzerland subsequently joined the Study Group.

Italian Government associated itself, asserting the need for larger economic units, and proclaiming its readiness "to enter into negotiations with all European Governments sharing these views who wish to enter a Customs Union with France and whose national economies are capable of being combined with the French economy in such a way as to make a viable unit." Greece and Turkey also declared their intention to study a "regional Customs Union" between these countries.

At the Committee Hearings in the House and the Senate on the Economic Cooperation Act of 1948—the Act under which European aid is being granted—every witness who referred in his testimony to customs union in Western Europe accepted movement toward customs union as both desirable in itself and as evidence of European willingness to move in the direction we wished of self-help through collective economic action. All who referred to customs union in the course of the Hearings—Cabinet Members, Senators, Congressmen, officials connected with the European Aid program, and other witnesses—were unanimous in treating Western European customs union in particular and customs union in general as patently desirable, and the only qualification that was suggested by anyone was that it should not be directed against the United States.[6] In the Congressional debates also, references to customs union seem to have been uniformly favorable.

The Economic Cooperation Act of 1948 makes no specific reference to customs union, but it provides that any country, to be eligible to receive assistance under the Act, must sign an

---

6. *Hearings before the Committee on Foreign Relations, United States Senate, Eightieth Congress, Second Session, on United States Assistance to European Economic Recovery, January, 1948; Hearings before the Committee on Foreign Affairs, House of Representatives, Eightieth Congress, Second Session, on United States Foreign Policy for a Post-War Recovery Program, February, 1948.* (In each case, see Index for references to "Customs Union.")

agreement with the United States which makes provision, among other things, for—

> cooperating with other participating countries in facilitating and stimulating an increasing interchange of goods and services among the participating countries and with other countries and cooperating to reduce barriers to trade among themselves and with other countries.[7]

In a speech made at Paris on October 31, 1949, before the Council of Economic Cooperation, Paul G. Hoffman, Administrator of the Economic Cooperation Administration, speaking no doubt with the approval of his government, clearly showed his disappointment at the failure of the Marshall Plan countries to make substantial progress toward the preferential removal among themselves of trade barriers. He made it clear that "economic integration" of Western Europe was an American objective not only as it might be instrumental in balancing Western Europe's trade with the dollar area but as desirable for its own sake as a means to long-run European prosperity. By "economic integration," he explained, he meant "the formation of a single large market within which quantitative restrictions on the movements of goods, monetary barriers to the flow of payments and, eventually, all tariffs are permanently swept away." He stated more clearly than had hitherto been done that this was from the first an objective of the Marshall Plan.

> This is a vital objective. It was to this that Secretary Marshall pointed in the speech which sparked Europe to new hope

---

7. United States, *Laws, Statutes,* etc., Public Law 472, 80th Congress, Chapter 169, 2d Session, S. 2202, Foreign Assistance Act of 1948, Approved April 3, 1948, Sec. 115(*b*)(3).

and new endeavor. It was on this promise [premise?] that the Congress of the United States enacted the ECA act. This goal is embodied in the convention of the OEEC.

Mr. Hoffman acknowledged that the full realization of such a program would encounter major difficulties, and accepted "close economic arrangements within one or more smaller groups of countries—always with the intention that these should contribute toward, and not be turned against, the integration of the whole of Western Europe and its overseas territories" as moves on the "path toward integration." He made it adequately clear that unless substantial progress was made along these lines there would be danger that the people and Congress of the United States would abandon the Marshall Plan.[8]

It is too early to tell whether any genuine progress is being made toward Western European customs union. The difficulties in the way are formidable, and if progress is made it is certain—in the absence of a major political crisis—to be gradual rather than climactic. On economic grounds, there can be little basis for reasonable doubt that the formation of a customs union embracing all or most of Western Europe, or even smaller customs unions which included at least several important countries with substantial overlapping in their ranges of heavily protected industries, would, in the net, contribute both to the economic recovery of Western Europe, once the necessary adjustments had been made, and to a greater degree of international specialization of production. The case, however, for smaller customs unions, except as steps towards the formation of large ones, if it can be made at all, must be made largely on other than economic grounds.

8. See the text of Mr. Hoffman's speech in the *New York Times,* November 1, 1949.

If all of Western Europe, or a large part of it, were to form a single customs union, it would become a more self-sufficing area as a whole—though its parts would become less self-sufficing than before. For the rest of the world, therefore, including the United States, its importance as an export market would probably decline, although if customs union brought greater prosperity to the area, as it should, this might more than offset the restrictive effect of the union on imports from outside the area of free trade. For the United States, however, the political and strategic interest in a stable and prosperous and strengthened Western Europe, and the economic interest in a Western Europe able to pay for the imports necessary to maintain its economic and political health, are clearly of much greater importance than the size of the market which Western Europe offers for American exports. Should the movement for customs union in Western Europe make rapid progress, however, it should be the American position that all friendly European countries should receive invitations to participate on equitable terms. The economic future of any European country which was left outside a Western European customs union and was also outside the Russian economic orbit would be grim indeed. Western European economic union would also result in there being left stranded unless rescued by the United States a number of non-European economic orphans. Whatever its merits, economic, political, strategic, moreover, Western European economic union launched under the inauspicious circumstances of open American pressure would carry forever a heavy burden of internal unpopularity.

The most pressing economic problem in the international field today is the problem of "dollar shortage," and some at least of the current drive for European customs union, or for preferential trade arrangements of other kinds, arises out of the belief or hope that it could provide at least a partial solution of this problem. In so far as the deficits in balances of payments of other countries in their trade with the United States can be attributed to inadequate export to the United States, customs union provides no solution whatsoever. In so far as these deficits are due to excessive imports from the United States, customs union provides a remedy of sorts. But to use customs union as a cure would be to make resort to more or less permanent and inflexible institutional changes, incapable of being accurately aimed even at the time of their institution at the appropriate target, to deal with a problem which by its nature is bound to be a temporary one in its location and intensity.

For the problem of "dollar shortage," the solution should be sought in measures which are less permanent in their nature, can be aimed better at the specific locations of dollar deficits, and can more easily be made available, technically, politically, and diplomatically. Measures of this character would be: devaluation of other currencies as compared to the dollar; anti-inflationary fiscal policies in countries with dollar deficits; the temporary exception, with American consent, of imports from the United States from obligations to refrain from discrimination in the application of trade barriers; unilateral reduction by the United States of its trade barriers; American financial aid to countries in balance-of-payments difficulties. Important steps have been taken in all five of these directions, in fact if not in form, in recent months, or earlier. The problem of "dollar shortage" should not be identified with the different, less tractable, and probably more lasting problem of shortage of the things purchasable most readily with dollars because of general deficiency of real buying power.

For the long-run problem of raising the level of economic well-being for the peoples of the world in general, customs union is only a partial, uncertain, and otherwise imperfect means of doing what world-wide non-discriminatory reduction of trade barriers can do more fully, more certainly, and more equitably, and it will be a sad outcome of confused thinking on our part if we in effect abandon our pursuit of the greater economic goal because of our fresh, and romantic, infatuation with the lesser goal.

3. Obstacles to the Formation of Customs Unions

Customs unions are not important, and are unlikely to yield more economic benefit than harm, unless they are between sizable countries which practice substantial protection of substantially similar industries. But customs unions of this character have always been extremely difficult to negotiate in a nationalistic and protectionist world. They have in recent times become more difficult to negotiate, for a variety of reasons.

Some of these reasons have already been discussed in this study, and can be here dealt with merely by mention. The disappearance of transit duties and the development as common practice of exempting imports for reexport from ordinary duties have removed one of the most important incentives as of a century ago to customs union. The program, under the International Trade Organization, for reduction of trade barriers on a universal basis, with strong sanction for concerted refusal to extend the benefit of these reductions to non-participating countries, plus the reform of American commercial policy, removes or at least weakens the incentive to multilateral preferential arrangements on a restricted territorial basis which American commercial policy provided until 1934. The absence of any approach to a world balance of power probably makes the political hazards for small countries of economic unification with large countries greater than they were in the nineteenth century. The Havana Charter makes other types of preferential tariff arrangements available without danger of retaliation from non-participating

countries—partial customs unions, interim agreements look-
ing toward the formation of customs unions, free-trade areas,
regional agreements, special agreements receiving International
Trade Organization approval. All of these are easier to negotiate
than complete customs union; most, if not all, of them can be
made to involve less intensification than customs union of competition with domestic industries; except for the possible administrative economies or political implications of complete customs
union, it is hard to find any weighty reason why that particular
form of preferential tariff arrangement should be sought, given
the commercial policy objectives of most countries, now that
alternative forms are at least equally available as far as external
sanctions are concerned.

There has occurred, moreover, since 1914, and especially since
the 1930's, a new development which makes the removal of trade
barriers between countries with important actual or potential
economic relations a much more formidable matter than it was
in the nineteenth century. This is the growth of governmental
intervention in industry, and especially of planned economies,
socialist or otherwise. In the nineteenth century, the free market
predominated, prices were flexible and unregulated, exchange
rates were relatively stable without need of exchange control,
and costs were not made rigid by wage regulation, social security programs, cartelization, or extensive collective bargaining.
Under these circumstances the removal of a tariff, while it might
cause temporary shock, could fairly rapidly be adjusted to, and all
that a tariff protected was the given allocation of resources. Now,
however, tariffs and other barriers to trade—quotas, import
licenses, exchange controls, state import monopolies, etc.—
protect not merely the allocation of employed resources but the
whole artificial national price and wage structures, the volume
of employment, the social security programs, the exchange rate
pegs, the monetary and fiscal policies, and so forth. There is no

longer any approach to international equilibrium of price structures, and what equilibrium there is in international balances of payments is for many countries dependent on the maintenance of appropriate barriers to imports, or subsidies to exports. Two neighboring countries contemplating complete customs union today must therefore contemplate also the necessity of harmonizing their general patterns of economic controls, which would involve a much more complete degree of economic unification than would a representative nineteenth-century customs union.

The same factors associated with planned economies which present obstacles to the formation of customs unions also make other types of removal or reduction of trade barriers more disturbing than they would have been under nineteenth-century conditions. There are, however, important differences of degree, if not of kind. In this connection, free-trade areas are closest to customs unions, but even here there is the difference that while participation in a free-trade area, as in a customs union, may result in deflationary pressure, an unfavorable balance of payments, and a tendency to unemployment, in the country with the relatively higher price- and money-cost structure, this country can offset this pressure under the free-trade area type of arrangement, by raising its tariff or other barriers against imports from outside the free-trade area, whereas under a customs union the common tariff would make this at least a more difficult and a slower remedy if it were available at all. Other types of preferential arrangements would leave the participating countries completely free to raise trade barriers against imports from outside as they pleased, and free within limits to maintain tariffs or other barriers to trade as between themselves. A substantial degree of divergence in monetary and fiscal policy, exchange rate policy, price structures, etc., could still be maintained as between such countries without being undermined by the free flow of goods between them. Whatever may be the strength of the economic case for uniformity for its own sake of economic policy for as large an area as possible—and, in the writer's opinion, there is an almost universal tendency to overestimate it and in any case to avoid critical examination of its merits and disadvantages—it is exceedingly difficult politically to negotiate it and to maintain it once negotiated unless it is brought about through a process of substantial political unification.

The economic case for removal of trade barriers, moreover, loses some of its logic when the setting is not that of one where prices and money-costs of production are determined by the free play of demand and supply in competitive markets. If the price structure is in important degree an artificial or arbitrary one, maintained by government supports and limitations or by official fiat, with only partial or no reference to the relations of supply to existing demand (or if there is private monopoly fixation of price), trade barriers may be necessary to protect a volume and direction of production which is appropriate to free-trade conditions but which cannot maintain itself against foreign competition at existing price- and money-cost levels. Under these circumstances, no government could conceivably agree to the total removal of all trade barriers as against imports from any country of commercial importance to it (unless there should be some country whose prices and money-costs were clearly higher and destined to remain higher indefinitely for most commodities which could compete in the absence of trade barriers with the products of domestic industries of critical importance), and in such a case it would be suicidal for the higher-price country to enter into such a union unless it was prepared to undertake a drastic deflation. Economic planning has made trade barriers protective of more than the allocation of resources and has thus made their removal a much more delicate and economically debatable matter. In so doing, it has made complete customs union, extending to all trade barriers and not merely to ordinary import duties, much more difficult to achieve. On the other hand, where the important trade barriers now take the form of import quotas and exchange controls rather than ordinary tariffs, the establishment of customs unions applying only to tariffs becomes easier, and unimportant.

Under existing conditions, the only type of substantial trade-barrier reduction which is feasible for a country which is not in a position of marked competitive advantage vis-à-vis the outside world—and the United States is the only important country which is today clearly in this position—is carefully measured reciprocal trade-barrier reduction which leaves it relatively in a balance-of-payments situation not substantially inferior to the preexisting one. This rules out customs union applying to all kinds of trade barriers between countries of comparative economic importance unless they are actually and potentially unimportant economically to each other or unless by chance pairs of countries can be found such that an appropriately chosen common external tariff will leave each member about where it was with respect to its aggregate balance of payments. This also rules out single bilateral bargains where concessions are subject to extension to third countries by virtue of the most-favored-nation clause, since this would tend to result in deficits—or increased deficits—in the balances of payments of both countries vis-à-vis the outside world. The only practical path, therefore, to trade-barrier reduction on most-favored-nation principles, as long as most economies are "planned," is the procedure sponsored by the Havana Charter of bilateral bargaining in a framework of multilateralism, with the right of third countries to claim the extension to themselves of the concessions made in the course of the bilateral bargaining open to them only if they have fully participated in the general bargaining.

In the international economic field, as in the field of international politics, this is a period of crisis. Effective solutions for crises are rarely easy to adopt or to execute. But if one looks only to the day, an apparently promising path to a solution can often be found whose first stages, if token in character, are fairly easy to pursue and whose later stages are pleasant to contemplate, though what is at its ultimate end is but a mirage. This, I fear, is the present-day role of customs union. Whether used as mere incantation against the evils resulting from present-day economic policy or vigorously prosecuted, it will in either case be unlikely to prove a practicable and suitable remedy for today's economic ills, and it will almost inevitably operate as a psychological barrier to the realization of the more desirable but less desired objectives of the Havana Charter—the balanced multilateral reduction of trade barriers on a non-discriminatory basis.

BIBLIOGRAPHY

Armitage-Smith, Sir Sydney. Report...on a Financial Mission to Tanganyika, September 26th, 1932. Presented by the Secretary of State for the Colonies to Parliament, October, 1932. British Parliamentary Papers, Cmd. 4182 (1932).

Ball, M. Margaret. *Post-War German-Austrian Relations: The Anschluss Movement, 1918–1936.* Stanford University, California: Stanford University Press, 1937.

Barrington, Daines. *Observations on the More Ancient Statutes.* 4th edition. London, 1775.

Beers, John S. de. "Tariff Aspects of a Federal Union," *Quarterly Journal of Economics* (Boston, Harvard University), Vol. 56 (1941), pp. 49–92.

Bell, Herbert C. F. *Lord Palmerston.* London: Longmans, Green & Company, 1936.

"Benelux, An Example of Unity in a Divided World," *Rotterdamsche Bank, Quarterly Review,* 1947, No. 4, pp. 5–42.

"Benelux and Industrial Development," *Amsterdamsche Bank, Quarterly Review,* No. 80, April, 1948, p. 15.

Bindoff, S. T. *The Scheldt Question to 1839.* London: George Allen & Unwin, 1945.

Bismarck, Otto von. *Correspondance diplomatique de M. de Bismarck (1851–1859), pub. d'après l'édition allemande de M. de Poschinger. Traduction de M. L. Schmitt.* Paris: E. Plon et Cie, 1883. II, 307 ff.; 423 ff.

—— *Die gesammelten Werke.* 2d edition. Berlin: O. Stolberg & Co., 1924–28. IV, 30–34.

Bismarck, the Man and the Statesman; Being the Reflections and Reminiscences of Otto Prince von Bismarck, Written and Dictated by Himself after his Retirement from Office. Translated from the

German under the supervision of A. J. Butler. London: Smith, Elder & Co., 1898. I, 377–78.

Bleuler, Werner. *Studien über Aussenhandel und Handelspolitik der Schweiz.* Zurich: Schulthess & Co., 1929.

Bosc, L. *Unions douanières et projets d'unions douanières.* Paris: A. Rousseau, 1904.

—— *Zollalliancen und Zollunionen in ihrer Bedeutung fuer die Handelspolitik der Vergangenheit und Zukunft.* German translation by S. Schilder. Berlin: Elwin Staude, 1907.

Brougham, Henry. "Balance of Power," *Works* (Edinburgh, 1872), VIII, 39.

Bruwer, A. J. *Protection in South Africa.* Stellenbosch: University of Pennsylvania, 1923.

Buchdahl, W. "The New 'Benelux' Union—Western European Tariff Pattern?" Project analyzed with special reference to Netherlands, Foreign Commerce Weekly (Washington), October 11, 1947, pp. 1–5, 32.

Buol-Schauenstein, K. F., and Cavour, C. B. *[Exchange of notes regarding the Customs Union beween Austria and Modena.]* Recueil des traités, conventions et actes diplomatiques concernant l'Autriche et l'Italie. Paris: Amyot, 1859. Pp. 731 ff.

Calmes, Albert. *Der Zollanschluss des Gross Herzogtums Luxemburg an Deutschland (1842–1918).* Luxemburg: Joseph Beffort, 1919.

Calwer, Richard. *Die Meistbegünstigung der Vereinigten Staaten von Nordamerika.* Berlin-Bern: Akademischer Verlag für social Wissenschaften, 1902.

Candolle, Augustin-Pyramus. *Mémoires et souvenirs.* Genève, 1862.

Chevalier, Michel. "La guerre et la crise européenne," *Revue des deux mondes* (Paris), XXXVI^2 (1866), 758–85.

Clémentel, Etienne. *La France et la politique économique interalliée.* Paris: Les Presses Universitaires de France, 1931.

Colban, Erik. *Mémoire sur la Convention Oslo. Carnegie Endowment Memorandum No. 1, International Studies Conference, 12th, Bergen, 1939.* Paris: International Institute of Intellectual Cooperation, 1939. Mimeographed.

Commission Mixte Franco-Italienne pour l'Etude d'une Union douanière entre la France et l'Italie. *Rapport final, Rome, le 22 décembre 1947.* Paris: Imprimerie Nationale, 1948. [The same published by the Istituto Poligrafico dello Stato, Rome, 1948; with Volume II: Annexes au Rapport final.]

—— *Compte rendu de la Commission Mixte Franco-Italienne d'Union Douanière, Paris, le 22 janvier 1949.* Paris: Imprimerie Nationale, 1949.

Committee of European Economic Cooperation. General Report, Paris, September 21, 1947. U. S. Department of State, Publication 2930. *See also below, under* Pan European Projects.

Davis, Kathryn W. *The Soviets at Geneva: The U.S.S.R. and the League of Nations, 1919–1933.* Geneva: Librairie Kundig, 1934.

Dechamps, A. "Une page d'histoire: Négotiations commerciales avec la France; Union douanière," *Revue générale (Bruxelles),* 1869, I, 540–69.

De Launoy, "Les projets d'union douanière franco-beige en 1841–42," *Revue catholique des idées et des faits (Bruxelles),* December, 1922.

Döberl, Michael. "Das Projekt einer Einigung Deutschlands auf wirtschaftlicher Grundlage a.d.J. 1665," *Forschungen zur Geschichte Bayerns,* VI (1898), 163–205. [Proposed union of Austria, Spain, Bavaria.]

Domerque, Gaston. "Le péril américain," *La réforme économique* (May 26 1901, February 2, 1902, June 15, 1902, etc.).

Drouyn de Lhuys, M. Livre jaune, 1864, p. 143.

East, W. G. *The Union of Moldavia and Wallachia, 1859: An Episode in Diplomatic History.* Cambridge, England: University Press, 1929.

Eisenmann, Louis. *Le compromis austro-hongrois de 1867: Etude sur le dualisme.* Paris: Bellais, 1904.

Elliott, O. L. *The Tariff Controversy in the United States, 1789–1833.* Palo Alto, California: Stanford University, 1892.

Evans, Ivor L. "Economic Aspects of Dualism in Austria-Hungary," *Slavonic Review (London),* VI (1927–28), 529–42.

Farnet, Gabriel. *Les relations douanières entre la France et la Principauté de Monaco.* Paris: Giard & Brière, 1917.

Federalist (The), [1777–1778], No. XI.

Fisk, George M. "Continental Opinion regarding a Proposed Middle European Tariff Union," *Johns Hopkins University Studies in Historical and Political Science,* Series XX, Nos. 11–12 (November–December, 1902). Baltimore: Johns Hopkins Press, 1902.

Fried, Alfred H. *The German Emperor and the Peace of the World.* New York: Hodder and Stoughton, 1912.

Funk, Martin Jos. *Die danzig-polnische Zollunion: Der bisherige und der künftige Zollverteilungs-schlüssel.* Jena: Gustav Fischer, 1926.

Gideonse, Harry D. "Economic Foundations of Pan-Europeanism," *Annals of the American Academy of Political and Social Science*, CXLIX (1930).

Giffen, Sir Robert. "The Dream of a British Zollverein," *Nineteenth Century* (London), May, 1902; reprinted in Giffen, *Economic Inquiries and Studies* (London, 1904), Vol. II, pp. 394–95.

Goforth, Wallace. "Canada's Economic Future," *International Journal (Quarterly of the Canadian Institute of International Affairs)*, III (1948), 285–308.

Gratz, Gustav, and Schüller, Richard. Die äussere Wirtschaftspolitik Oesterreich-Ungarns, Mitteleuropäische Pläne. *Carnegie Stiftung fuer Internationalen Frieden, Abteilung für Volkswirtschaft und Geschichte.* Vienna: Hölder-Pichler-Tempsky, A. G.; New Haven: Yale University Press, 1925.

—— The Economic Policy of Austria-Hungary during the War in its External Relations. English version by W. Alison Phillips. *Carnegie Endowment for International Peace: Division of Economics and History.* New Haven: Yale University Press, 1928.

Gregory, T. E. *Tariffs: A Study in Method.* London: Griffin, 1921.

Grunzel, Josef. *Handelspolitik und Ausgleich in Österreich-Ungarn.* Wien und Leipzig: Alfred Hölder, 1912.

Guizot, F. P. J. Mémoires pour servir à l'histoire de mon temps. *Paris-Leipzig*, 1858–1867. VI, 276–96.

Haberler, Gottfried von. "The Political Economy of Regional or Continental Blocs," *in* Seymour E. Harris, *ed., Postwar Economic Problems* (New York: McGraw-Hill, 1943).

——The Theory of International Trade with its Applications to Commercial Policy. London: Macmillan & Co., Ltd., 1936.

Halle, Ernst von. "Das Interesse Deutschlands an der amerikanischer Präsidentenwahl des Jahres 1896," *Jahrbuch für Gesetzgebung, Verwaltung, und Volkswirtschaft ("Schmollers Jahrbuch")*, New Series, XX (1896), 263–96.

Havana Charter for an International Trade Organization, March 24, 1948. U. S. Department of State, Commercial Policy Series 114.

Hawtrey, R. G. *Economic Destiny.* London: Longmans, Green & Company, 1944.

Helmreich, E. C. *The Diplomacy of the Balkan Wars, 1912–1913.* Cambridge, Massachusetts: Harvard University Press, 1938.

Henderson, William Otto. *The Zollverein.* Cambridge: University Press, 1939.

International Chamber of Commerce. 6th Congress, Washington, 1931. [Papers presented to the Congress, No. 12.] Exceptions to the Most Favoured Nation Treatment. Replies of National Committees and Memorandum on Dr. Richard Riedl's Report. Paris: Herbert Clarke, 1931.

The International Conferences of American States, 1889–1928. *Carnegie Endowment for International Peace.* New York: Oxford University Press, 1931.

The International Conferences of American States: First Supplement, 1933–1940. Washington: Carnegie Endowment for International Peace, 1940.

International Studies Conference. 6th, London, 1933. *The State and Economic Life.* Paris: International Institute of Intellectual Cooperation, 1934.

Ito, N. *La clause de la nation la plus favorisée.* Paris: Les Editions Internationales, 1930.

Jánossy, Dionys. "Der handelspolitische Konflikt zwischen der Österreichischungarischen Monarchie und Serbien in den Jahren 1904–1910," *Jahrbuch des wiener ungarischen historischen Instituts (Budapest),* Vol. II (1932), 285–312.

Keith, Theodora. "Commercial Relations of England and Scotland, 1663–1707." Girton College Studies No. 1, Cambridge, England, 1910.

—— "The Economic Causes for the Scottish Union," *English Historical Review (London),* XXIV (1909), 44–60.

Kobatsch, Rudolf. *La politique économique internationale.* Paris, 1913.

League of Nations. *Commercial Policy in the Interwar Period: International Proposals and National Policies,* Geneva, 1942. Publication II. Economic and Financial, 1942.II.A.6. Pp. 52–60.

—— *Commission of Enquiry for European Union. Minutes of the Third Session of the Commission, May 15–21, 1931.* Document C.395.M.158.1931. VII. Pp. 16–24, 79–88.

—— *Economic Committee. Equality of Treatment in the Present State of International Commercial Relations,* Geneva, 1936. Document C.379.M.250. 1936.II.B.

—— *Remarks on the Present Phase of International Economic Relations, September 1937.* Document C.358.M.242.1937.II.B. Pp. 14–15.

—— *Journal of the Monetary and Economic Conference.* London, 1933.

—— *Monetary and Economic Conference. Draft Annotated Agenda Submitted by the Preparatory Commission of Experts.* Geneva, 1933. League Document C.48.M.18.1933.II. Conference Document M.E.I.

—— *Reports Approved by the Conference on July 27th, 1933, and Resolutions Adopted by the Bureau and the Executive Committee.* London, 1933. League Document C.435.M.220.1933.II. Conference Document M.E. 22 (1).

—— *Official Journal, 1931.* (On the Anschluss controversy.)

—— *Permanent Mandates Commission. Minutes of the Ninth Session.* Geneva, 1926. Pp. 98–101.

—— *Recommendations of the Economic Committee relating to Commercial Policy.* Geneva, 1929. Document C.138.M.53.1929.II.

—— *Recommendations of the Economic Committee relating to Tariff Policy and the Most-Favoured-Nation Clause.* Document E.805. Publication II. Economic and Financial, 1933, II.B.1. P. 21.

—— *Report and Proceedings of the World Economic Conference, Geneva, 1927.* Document C.356.M.129.1927.II. Vol. II, p. 152.

—— Secretariat. See below under United Nations...Customs Unions (1947); for additional references to L.N. documents, see Bibliography therein.

Leubuscher, Charlotte. *Tanganyika Territory: A Study of Economic Policy under Mandate.* London: Oxford University Press, 1944.

List, Friedrich. *The National System of Political Economy [1841].* Sampson S. Lloyd, tr. New York: Longmans, Green & Company, 1904.

Litschi, Joseph. "Das Retorsions-Konkordat vom Jahre 1822," *Zeitschrift für schweizerische Statistik (Bern)*, XXVIII (1892), 1–22.

Lončarević, Dusān. *Jugoslaviens Entstehung.* Zurich, 1929.

Mantoux, Etienne. *The Carthaginian Peace; or The Economic Consequences of Mr. Keynes.* New York: Oxford University Press, 1946.

Masson, Henry. *Les unions douanières.* (Extract from Report of the Congrès International d'Expansion Economique Mondiale, held at Mons, Belgium, 1905.)

Masters, Donald C. *The Reciprocity Treaty of 1854: Its History, its Relation to British Colonial and Foreign Policy and to the Development of Canadian Fiscal Autonomy.* London: Longmans, Green & Company, 1937.

Matlekovits, Sandor von. *Die Zollpolitik der österreichisch-ungarischen Monarchie und des Deutschen Reiches seit 1868 und deren nächste Zukunft.* Leipzig: Duncker und Humbolt, 1891.

Melder, Frederick E. *State and Local Barriers to Interstate Commerce in the United States.* Orono, Maine, 1937.

Mills, Stephen. *Taxation in Australia.* London: Macmillan and Co., Limited, 1925.

Molinari, G. de. "Union douanière de l'Europe central," *Journal des économistes*. Vol. 5, Series 4, February 1879, pp. 309–18.

National Foreign Trade Council. *European Economic Alliances*. New York, 1916.

Newton, A. P., ed. *Select Documents relating to the Unification of South Africa*. London: Longmans, Green and Co., 1924.

Ninth International Conference of American States (1948). See below, United States, Department of State.

Oncken, Auguste. "L'Article onze du Traité de Paix de Francfort," *Revue d'économie politique (Paris)*, V (1891), 602.

Peez, Alexander von. "A propos de la situation douanière en Europe," *Revue d'économie politique (Paris)*, V (1891).

—— *Die Amerikanische Konkurrenz*. Leipzig, 1881.

Pentmann, J. *Die Zollunionsidee und ihre Wandlungen im Rahmen der wirtschaftspolitischen Ideen und der Wirtschaftspolitik des 19. Jahrhunderts bis zur Gegenwart*. Jena: Gustav Fischer, 1917.

Permanent Court of International Justice. *Customs Régime between Germany and Austria. Series C. Pleadings, Oral Statements, and Documents. XXIId Session, 1931, No. 53*.

Poel, Jean van der. *Railway and Customs Policies in South Africa, 1885–1910*. London: Longmans, Green & Company, 1933.

Potter, Pitman B. "Universalism versus Regionalism in International Organization," *American Political Science Review*, XXXVII (1943).

Rappard, William E. "Post-War Efforts for Freer Trade," *Geneva Studies*, IX (1938), No. 2.

Richelot, Henri. *L'Association douanière allemande*. Paris, 1845.

Ridder, Alfred de. *Les projets d'union douanière franco-beige et les puissances européennes (1836–1843)*. Bruxelles: Lamertin, 1933.

Riedl, Richard. *Exceptions to the Most-Favored-Nation Treatment*. Report Presented to the International Chamber of Commerce. London: P. S. King & Son, Ltd., 1931.

Robbins, Lionel C. *Economic Planning and International Order*. London: Macmillan and Co., Ltd., 1937.

Salis, Jean R. de. *Sismondi, 1773–1842: Lettres et documents inédits*. Paris: H. Champion, 1932.

Schmoller, Gustav. "Die Handels- und Zoll- annäherung Mitteleuropas," *Jahrbuch für Gesetzgebung, Verwaltung, und Volkswirtschaft im Deutschen Reich (Schmollers Jahrbuch)*, XL (1916).

Schwarzenberger, Georg. "The Most-Favored-Nation Standard in British State Practice," *British Year Book of International Law,* 1945 (London, 1946), pp. 96–121.

Scott, W. R. "The Fiscal Policy of Scotland before the Union," *Scottish Historical Review (Glasgow),* I (1904), 173–90.

Sieghart, Rudolf. *Zolltrennung und Zolleinheit: Die Geschichte der österreichisch-ungarischen Zwischenzoll-linie.* Wien: Manz, 1915.

Smith, Adam. *An Inquiry into the Nature and Causes of the Wealth of Nations [1776], Cannan edition.* London: Methuen & Co., 1904.

Smith, R. Elberton. *Customs Valuation in the United States: A Study in Tariff Administration.* Chicago: University of Chicago Press, 1948.

Snyder, Richard C. *The Most-Favored-Nation Clause: An Analysis with Particular Reference to Recent Treaty Practice and Tariffs.* New York: King's Crown Press, 1948.

Spengler, Joseph J. "Regional Differences and the Future of Manufacturing in America," *Southern Economic Journal* (Chapel Hill, North Carolina), VII (1941), 475–81.

Story, Joseph. Commentaries on the Constitution. *Sections* 1056–1073.

Théry, Edmond. *Europe et Etats-Unis d'Amérique.* Paris: E. Flammarion, 1899.

Transvaal. *Report of the Customs and Industries Commission. Presented to both houses of Parliament by command of His Excellency the Governor.* Pretoria: Government Printing and Stationery Office, 1908.

The Treaties of Peace, 1919–1923. New York: Carnegie Endowment for International Peace, 1924.

Treitschke, H. von. "Aus den Papieren des Staats-ministers von Motz," *Preussische Jahrbücher (Berlin),* XXXIX (1877), 412–14.

Trotter, R. G. *Canadian Federation: Its Origins and Achievements: A Study in Nation Building.* Toronto, London: Dent and Sons, 1924.

United Nations, Department of Economic Affairs. *Customs Unions: A League of Nations Contribution to the Study of Customs Union Problems.* Lake Success, New York, 1947. (For additional references to L.N. documents, see its Bibliography, pp. 96–97.)

United States Congress. House Committee on Foreign Affairs. Hearings...*Eightieth Congress, Second Session, on United States Foreign Policy for a Post-War Recovery Program.... February, 1948.* Washington: Government Printing Office, 1948.

United States Congress. Select Committee on Foreign Aid, Subcommittee on France and the Low Countries. *Preliminary Report Twenty-Four. The Belgian-Luxemburg-Netherlands Customs and*

Economic Union [Benelux]. April, 1948. Washington: Government Printing Office, 1948.

United States Congress. Senate Committee on Foreign Relations. *Hearings...Eightieth Congress, Second Session, on United States Assistance to European Economic Recovery...January, 1948.* Washington: Government Printing Office, 1948.

United States Congress. *Journals of the Continental Congress, 1774–1789.* Edited from the original records in the Library of Congress. W. C. Ford and Gaillard Hunt, *eds.* Washington: Government Printing Office, 1904–37. XXV, 628–30; 661–64.

United States Department of Commerce. Bureau of Foreign and Domestic Commerce. *Bibliography of Barriers to Trade between States.* Washington: Government Printing Office, 1942.

United States Department of State. *The Revolutionary Diplomatic Correspondence of the United States,* Francis Wharton, *ed.* Washington: Government Printing Office, 1889. VI, 691.

United States Congress. Ninth International Conference of American States, Bogotá, Colombia, March 30–May 2, 1948; Report of the Delegation of the United States of America, with Related Documents. Publication 3263.

United States Congress. Laws, Statutes, etc. Public Law 472, 80th Congress, Chapter 169, 2d Session, S. 2202. Foreign Assistance Act of 1948. Approved April 3, 1948, Sec. 115 (*b*) (3).

United States Tariff Commission. *Colonial Tariff Policies.* Washington: Government Printing Office, 1922.

United States Tariff Commission. *Dictionary of Tariff Information.* Washington: Government Printing Office, 1924. Pp. 356 ff.

United States Tariff Commission. *Reciprocity and Commercial Treaties.* Washington: Government Printing Office, 1919. Pp. 416–44.

Viner, Jacob. "The Measurement of the 'Height' of Tariff Levels," *The Improvement of Commercial Relations between Nations,* Joint Committee, Carnegie Endowment-International Chamber of Commerce (Paris, 1936), pp. 58–68.

—— "The Most-Favored-Nation Clause," *Index (Svenska Handelsbanken, Stockholm),* VI (1931), p. 11.

—— "The Most-Favored-Nation Clause in American Commercial Treaties," *Journal of Political Economy* (University of Chicago), XXXII (1924), 101–29.

Wilcox, Clair. *A Charter for World Trade.* New York: The Macmillan Company, 1949.

INDEX